CREATE, PERFORM, TEACH!

of related interest

Storytelling and Story-Reading in Early Years
How to Tell and Read Stories to Young Children
Mary Medlicott
ISBN 978 1 78592 298 5
eISBN 978 1 78450 604 9

Supporting Toddlers' Wellbeing in Early Years Settings
Strategies and Tools for Practitioners and Teachers
Edited by Helen Sutherland and Yasmin Mukadam
ISBN 978 1 78592 262 6
eISBN 978 1 78450 552 3

Developing Empathy in the Early Years
A Guide for Practitioners
Helen Garnett
ISBN 978 1 78592 143 8
eISBN 978 1 78450 418 2

Promoting Emotional Wellbeing in Early Years Staff
A Practical Guide for Looking after
Yourself and Your Colleagues
Sonia Mainstone-Cotton
ISBN 978 1 78592 335 7
eISBN 978 1 78450 656 8

Learning through Movement and
Active Play in the Early Years
A Practical Resource for Professionals and Teachers
Tania Swift
ISBN 978 1 78592 085 1
eISBN 978 1 78450 346 8

School Readiness and the Characteristics
of Effective Learning
The Essential Guide for Early Years Practitioners
Tamsin Grimmer
ISBN 978 1 78592 175 9
eISBN 978 1 78450 446 5

CREATE, PERFORM, TEACH!

An Early Years Practitioner's Guide to Developing Your Creativity and Performance Skills

NIKKY SMEDLEY

Illustrations by Sam Greaves

Jessica Kingsley *Publishers*
London and Philadelphia

First published in 2018
by Jessica Kingsley Publishers
73 Collier Street
London N1 9BE, UK
and
400 Market Street, Suite 400
Philadelphia, PA 19106, USA

www.jkp.com

Library of Congress Cataloging in Publication Data
Names: Smedley, Nikky, author.
Title: Create, perform, teach! : an early years practitioner's guide to
   developing your creativity and performance skills / Nikky Smedley.
Description: London ; Philadelphia : Jessica Kingsley Publishers, 2019. |
   Includes index.
Identifiers: LCCN 2018006134 | ISBN 9781785924316 (alk. paper)
Subjects: LCSH: Education, Preschool--Activity programs. | Creative
   activities and seat work. | Storytelling. | Acting games. | Role playing.
   | Puppet theater.
Classification: LCC LB1140.35.C74 S54 2019 | DDC 372.21--
dc23 LC record available at https://lccn.loc.gov/2018006134

British Library Cataloguing in Publication Data
A CIP catalogue record for this book is available from the British Library

ISBN 978 1 78592 431 6
eISBN 978 1 78450 799 2

Printed and bound by CPI Group (UK) Ltd, Croydon, CR0 4YY

For my mother, to give her a
simple answer to the question,
'So what's Nikky up to these days?'

Contents

INTRODUCTION

Hello and welcome to *Create, Perform, Teach!* – a practical guide to help EYFS (Early Years Foundation Stage) practitioners adapt creative and performance techniques and skills for the classroom.

There may not seem to be a particularly obvious correlation between the working life of a professional performer and that of an EYFS practitioner, but there are a surprising number of parallels.

Through using this book, you will be able to develop activities that cover the three different ways that children learn, as laid down in the EYFS Statutory Framework. These are, as you know: playing and exploring; active learning; and creating and thinking critically – not just characteristics of effective teaching and learning, but essentials in the toolkit of any performer!

Let me start by telling you a little bit about myself and how this book came to be.

I started my career as a professional dancer, performing for other choreographers as well as creating my own work for my own company. We endeavoured to push the boundaries of accessibility, making dance theatre that we hoped would appeal to new audiences – families and children as well as the regular arts crowd. We mixed it up a bit, including singing, cabaret, comedy and some pretty outlandish costumes, but we also made some serious points through our dances. Alongside the performing, I also taught in vocational institutions such as the Laban Centre and Lewisham College. But a girl can only dance for so long, and as my body and bank balance started to feel that the pain was a little too great to continue, I lucked out with a job in children's television, playing Laa-Laa in *Teletubbies*. This move was to influence the rest of my life.

The programme was put together with such care, such knowledge of and love for small children, that I was hooked. I became fascinated with what was meaningful for our little ones, and endeavoured to learn as much as I possibly could from the geniuses at Ragdoll who were now my bosses. Part of their methodology was to go out and spend time with young children for research purposes, and as I moved from performing into writing, directing and producing, to this end, I began holding movement workshops in local nurseries and schools. As the years rolled on, I started to enjoy the time I spent with real live children more than I enjoyed making television for them. So after a brief period of re-training, I became a freelance creative educational practitioner, working in EYFS, primary, secondary and

SEN (Special Education Needs) settings over the next two decades.

Alongside this work I also started writing and performing my own children's stories, and I created and toured theatre pieces for young children and their families. As these two threads of work – the educational and the theatrical – developed in tandem, I began to see how much they were linked. So I started to bring the skills that I had learned and embedded, over my many years in theatre and television, into the classroom, and I found them especially pertinent to the EYFS setting.

Now my life is much more taken up with the written and spoken word. I continue to write and tell stories for young children, I write for educational magazines, I blog for the 'How to Speak Child' initiative and I give live presentations around communication with, for and by children. So it seemed like the right time (the write time?!) to put what I have learned over the years into a book.

I have tried to give you a mixture of practical suggestions that you can apply straight away, case studies to show how it *might* turn out and some deeper theory and reflection. I also hope it's a fun read! At the end of every chapter I have extracted three 'kernels', as an attempt to sum up the essence of that chapter in a few pithy phrases that you can easily remember at your work.

Although each chapter has a specific focus, the activities and points discussed tend towards the multi-faceted, enabling you the practitioner to provide learning opportunities that cover the varied learning proclivities of the children you have in your care. These creative modes of teaching and learning can ensure that – without making differentiation arduous – visual, kinaesthetic and aural elements are included in any activity. Due to their holistic nature, each subject will almost always cover more than one of the three prime areas specified in the EYFS, and in the main this should be fairly obvious, but where appropriate, I will give a more detailed indication of where the subject matter attaches to the EYFS Framework.

The most important element in all this, however, is you.

This is a book that is focussed on you and your development; it's not *just* full of stuff for the kids to do. It's about the importance of what you the practitioner bring to the classroom, and to your relationships with your children. It's also about how your increased ability and confidence in the skills normally associated with performers – storytelling, puppetry, music, movement and more – can benefit you directly, as well as the children you teach.

In the world of performance, the audience is the most important thing, but unless the actors know how to act, the dancers know how to dance, the musicians can play, the singers can sing, then the audience can have a pretty grim time. It's the same in the classroom. Naturally, the children's needs are paramount, but the more skills the practitioner has to draw from, the happier and more confident they will feel in their ability to deliver, and so the more the children will get out of the experience.

We all know that a happy child is a learning child. We know that children learn much less well from someone that they don't like – or even worse, who they feel doesn't like them – therefore it makes sense to make happy practitioners too.

So – let's start at the very beginning, let's start with you...

Chapter 1

WHO IS IT?

Personal honesty is important; it's what's needed to make performance — and anything else — believable. So how do you bring your whole self to the classroom, modelling truthfulness and encouraging your children to feel safe enough to do the same themselves?

In the same way that children are often more likely to open up to an aunty or grandpa than they are to a parent, as a visiting creative practitioner, I've enjoyed being a sounding board for very many school children in many different settings. Within the various whinges and moans, I've been able to detect consistencies that seem to hold across age, sex, race, geography — well, across all variables actually. Chief of these is a desire for their teachers to be completely honest with them.

I'm not talking about whether or not teachers are telling lies, of course, but about a level of personal honesty

– about bringing the whole of oneself to the party. Even very young children are extremely sensitive to this issue.

When we start to think about it, it makes perfect sense. A person who is open and relaxed about who they are portrays a level of confidence, of belief in their own competence, and that makes us feel secure. It's only when people are anxious, nervous, or doubt their own capabilities that they find it necessary to hide behind a facade. So if we feel that a person is keeping something from us, we pick up on their discomfort and that makes us feel insecure too.

There's also a cultural norm which tells us that when we are in a position of authority, we must assume command, and in no way let any chink in our armour, or the slightest vulnerability, be detected. We are encouraged to cultivate a mask of invincibility behind which we must hide our imperfect selves. This is especially true when we are in charge of a group of children.

It's difficult to be the grown-up in the room sometimes. There can be a huge pressure to be able to deal with absolutely everything, to know everything, to be able to maintain control whilst giving space for personal expression, to be perfect at our job. But that's impossible. We are all fallible, and it's important that we make peace with that. Whilst we are striving daily to give of our best, it's also okay not to have the answer sometimes; we are allowed to say, 'I don't know.' To be able to model this for our children is crucial. As they grow and develop through their school careers, they are going to be subjected to terrific pressures themselves. They need to learn that on the occasions when they don't know a thing, or they are stuck in some way – they don't need to panic. They too can just say, 'I don't know', and that's all right. Once they have seen the adults they admire behave in this way without drama or self-abasement, then they are more likely to be able to do the same themselves. After all, the admittance of ignorance is also the starting point for exploratory learning: 'Let's find out together!'

Some of the children that come into your care will have had a limited amount of exposure to grown-ups, sometimes rarely coming into contact with any adults who are not part of their immediate family. The more you can show them that you are a multi-faceted human being with positives and negatives just like them, then the more you are giving them validation of self. Whether you like it or not, you are a role model!

This is really where the inspiration for this book comes from. There's a lot of common ground between your role as an EYFS practitioner and that of a creative performer. For at least part of the day, you will find yourself in front of your tiny audience, trying to hold their interest and obtain the responses and behaviours you desire. Sometimes as actor, sometimes director or even conductor. Like all audiences they will be unpredictable, they will let their feelings be known and, most of all, they will know if you're faking it. If nothing else, you have to be believable.

When I am holding workshops for trainee teachers, I use the same phrase as when I am working with drama students:

'It's all about commitment.'

That doesn't mean that you have to go hell-for-leather into everything, nor does it mean you have to work yourself into the ground. It just means that you have to give your whole self, your whole attention to every moment and whatever that moment requires. You have to mean it.

The most successful teachers I have worked with manage to engender in their classes a sense of team. Their children think of themselves as part of a cohesive group to which they, their peers and the associated adults belong. They hold an idea of the collective personality of the group and feel a responsibility to the overall success of that group. In order to achieve this, there must be an acknowledgement that the group needs each and every individual, that everyone has a part to play and all are reliant on all the other members of the group to pull their weight. As the teacher, to be able to ask for assistance on occasion gives a feeling of usefulness and belonging to the children and helps to cement that commitment to the group.

Again, there are parallels to be drawn here with what is necessary to create a successful performance. Cast and crew are brought together for a production and are expected to form a cohesive company, committing to each other and to the common goal as fully as possible.

I have been on both sides of this process – as a cast member of somebody else's company, and as an artistic director, needing to pull together my own company in order to succeed – and there are valuable lessons that I've learned along the way, which have also served me in good stead in the classroom.

For a common goal to be achieved, everyone has to be aware of what that goal is. If you are creating a new show, then there has to be some consensus; about whether it's dance or circus or a play or a mixture of forms; about who it's for, and where it will be performed; about how many people are in it, when and where it's set and so forth. In a classroom, you should be clear about the atmosphere you want to create, about the overall style of your teaching, and about what success looks like to you.

Communication is key. In film and television everyone is given a call sheet every evening, with relevant contact details and the shooting schedule for the following day. I'm not suggesting for a minute that you adopt this as a procedure; however, the principle is sound. That everyone who needs to know what's going on is given the information they require. For example, once you have decided what your common goal will be, make sure everyone is aware of it, maybe make a sign together, perhaps make up a rhyme, a song or a motto for your class – your team. These kinds of things can be hugely helpful when it comes to building a group identity, a common bond. Little rituals to deal with everyday tasks can similarly lead to a shared experience and sense of community, as well as getting the job done.

⁓⁓⁓⁓⁓⁓

During one autumn term, I worked with a nursery group who really struggled with the whole rigmarole of getting ready to go outside. Some children would bypass the cloakroom altogether, impatiently racing into the playground only to find themselves shivering minutes later, complaining to the staff on duty about the cold and needing to go back inside to get more clothes. Others struggled with the order of events, putting gloves on before anything else, rendering themselves more than a little ham-fisted when it came to coat fastenings and wellies. More often than not, there would be children who had taken all of break time coping with getting wrapped up, only to find time had run out and it was time to take it all off again. It also took up a lot of staff effort, without much reward.

So we made up a little song with actions:

It's cold outside
We're going outside
What do we need to do?
Let's start now!

We're pulling on our boots – Stompy Stompy Stomp!
We're putting on our coats – Zip Zip Zippity Zip!
We're putting on our scarves – Winding Round and Round!
We're pulling on our hats – Nice. And. Tight.
and last of all...
and last of all...
On go our gloves – our favourite gloves.
We're all wrapped up
Let's go outside!

In order not to cause *complete* chaos in the cloakroom, we sang the song and did the actions in the classroom beforehand. In that way, the children were reminded about what they had to do in advance of actually doing it. It only took a few minutes, and helped reduce the confusion when they got to the job proper.

Now I realise it's no great work of art – but it was effective.

~~~~~~~~~~

Rituals help children remember what it is they should be doing. They can incorporate rhyme, rhythm and repetition, music, movement, all of these or none of them. They are useful for marking out the regular occasions of the day, or the week, for giving praise or thanks, or celebrating. Best of all, you can make them up together. I've found that a 'welcome' ritual can be really bonding and very warming for the children – whether it's performed at the beginning of the day, to visitors, or most importantly when a new child joins the group and you want to help them feel part of the team as soon as they are able.

This also touches on the importance of routine. The proper order of things can be applied to a longer period of time – which in theatre would be read-throughs, then rehearsals, then technicals, then dress rehearsals, then performance. There's also the daily routine – to follow the TV example, that would be warm-ups, then pick-ups, then rehearsals, then shooting. Routine allows the practicalities for any group to function as smoothly as possible, and it's a truism to say that children need that consistency. You will need it too, but within that framework, allow yourself some flexibility for the unforeseen, and again –

don't panic. There will be certain timings and events you have to incorporate into your day, but the important thing to remember is that you do have some choice. Aside from the certain constraints within which you have to work, you are free to create a routine that ties in with your overall vision.

So we already have a surprisingly large amount of ways in which the lives of an EYFS practitioner and that of a creative performer are similar, and we have several transferable lessons. Here are a few more techniques I have borrowed from the theatre and applied to the classroom:

- Having clear roles – Children love to be given responsibility, so if there are regular little tasks that need taking care of, put someone in charge of each one, perhaps for a week at a time.

- Warm-up and trust exercises – A short physical warm-up to get the day started can work well, and if it does so for you, then try adding in movements where the children have to rely on each other (sitting leaning back to back for example) to help with co-operation skills.

- Rehearsals – We mostly don't get it right first time around. Let everyone know that that's okay, and that practising can be as worthwhile as achieving the goal.

- We all contribute – Create an atmosphere in which everyone feels safe enough to make a contribution. Performers lay themselves on the line all the time;

it's very exposing. We should remember that small children can feel that way too.

- Applaud – Give praise sincerely and often. Encouragement is one of the top factors for building good learners. Help your children to recognise and acknowledge achievement in one another and use praise to build that group feeling.

Most of all, make it fun! Your children should *want* to be part of the gang, to be proud to be a member of the group, of your class. And, whilst being an integral part of the whole, let them know that they also have room for their own personalities. Yes, you want them to contribute, they may at times have to comply, but they don't have to conform or compromise their personalities in order to be accepted.

Which brings me back to YOU!

~~~~~~~~~~

A practitioner exercise I regularly use is to ask everyone to work on their own to write a list of things they do in their spare time. Absolutely any interest, activity or source of enjoyment is acceptable. We then put the lists aside and work together as a group to draw up a list of areas from the EYFS Framework that the teachers are keen to concentrate on in their classes.

Then we bring the personal lists back and work in pairs to apply the outside interest to the demands of the curriculum.

There can be some really wonderfully creative ideas. My favourite was a lady who attended weekly flamenco classes, and suddenly realised that she had at her disposal a way of teaching counting that was engaging, multi-sensory, fun and effective!

We all have elements of our lives that we've maybe not thought about using in our practice. For me, bringing Pilates exercise bands to nursery was a revelation – this is something of what I mean by bringing your whole self to the party.

Try the exercise for yourself. Have a think about what other skills or quirks or party tricks you have up your sleeve that you can apply to your teaching.

Performers draw on their entire personal toolkit to do the best job possible, and it's a technique that really works in the classroom. Apart from anything else, it makes it a whole lot more fun.

~~~~~~~~~~~

A colleague of mine who specialises in making theatre for children, and who also holds workshops for her young audiences, talks about what she called the 'Body Shop Moment'. That moment when you're all set up and ready, waiting for the children to arrive, that short moment of peace before 30–60 little people are in front of you waiting for something wonderful to happen. She says in that moment she wonders why she does what she does. Because it's hard, and it's scary. Not because she's frightened of the children, but because she's anxious about letting them down, she really wants them to enjoy themselves and get something out of the occasion – and wouldn't it be easier to just go and get a job in Body Shop. She'd probably smell better too!

But of course she does it for a reason, and she mostly loves it while it's happening, like yourself.

You know that the most important thing you can bring is your positive energy, and when you feel good, it's easy. But no one is super human, you're not going to feel good all of the time, so what do you do when it's a bit harder to dig deep? After all, your children don't really care about what's going on with you, outside of their immediate experience – nor should they, they're kids, that's not their job.

The best advice I can give is to know yourself. Know yourself and what works best for you. You need to still be able to do your job, and to bring that positive energy even when you're feeling rubbish, so you need to have a couple of techniques up your sleeve to cope with the 'Body Shop Moment' – and more besides. The show *must* go on!

You may already know exactly what you need to do in that circumstance. It took me a while to figure out what works for me – it's not rocket science, but I needed to be able to have a succinct mantra to repeat whilst I was taking a deep breath and preparing to carry on, and here it is:

Remember why you went into this.

There's no need for you to know exactly why I did, but it came about from what I learned working in children's television, and how that inspired me to move into education.

I was totally unprepared for how tired I would get when I was a Teletubby. Previously I'd been a professional dancer, which was no walk in the park effort-wise, but I had never worked so physically hard for so many consecutive hours, never sweated so much, never carried so much weight around, never been so oxygen deprived whilst working. In short – it was tough.

I needed something to hold onto, something to motivate me when I felt like my deepest energy reserves were depleted. What I did was to think of the child. To think of the child who had been put in front of the television whilst the adult saw to some of the day's tasks. A child who needed love and laughter and warmth, regardless of how I felt. Like I said, that child doesn't care about what is going on in my life, doesn't care how tired I am, and deserves my best efforts regardless.

You will have your own reasons, you will know why you went into teaching EYFS – there is a base from which all your practice grows, a spring from which it flows. Access that, put it into words, into a short phrase and keep it with you like a charm for when the exhaustion and frustration hits.

This book is for you, because you have chosen to do something wonderful and amazing, but something that will take the best you have to offer, and that needs to take it every day.

I hope it is a book that will help the true you shine through for your children. I'm interested in your health and well-being, your skill set and your motivation, because you need to be at your peak in order to benefit the children in your care, because that care is priceless.

THE KERNELS

- Honestly bring your whole self to the party.

- Build your team and develop a sense of group identity.

- Find your 'Why?' Use it to motivate yourself when times get tough.

Chapter 2

STRUCTURING THE CLASS FOR PHYSICALITY

Let's acknowledge the physical needs of young children. Here are some techniques to accommodate these needs whilst maintaining smooth running of the day.

Small children are inherently physical beings. They have not yet been conditioned to think of their bodies as separate from their brains and so they experience everything with their whole selves. They are right to do so, as they are learning all the time not just with their brains, not just with their five senses, but with every part of them.

So we need to take this on board. As I've said before, my background as a physical performer was my first way in to teaching, and I started out by holding movement workshops. Later on in the book, we'll look specifically at movement and dance activities you can give your children, but here I want to look at the bigger picture and how you can bring physicality into the wider structure of the classroom and the school day.

When you first get into a new classroom, take some time to really study the environment and how the children move around within it. Of course there are all kinds of studies and many experts on the design of EYFS learning spaces, as well as those whose business it is to sell as many products into schools as possible. This can lead to conflicting ideas and pieces of advice which are tricky to negotiate, and which on occasion end in out-and-out disaster. I worked in one school which had spent a fortune on an architect-led refurbishment. Everything looked absolutely beautiful, but it had been constructed from an architect's perspective, not from a child's. Consequently some hideous errors had been made – not least of which were the very attractive curved tables and benches which were concreted into floor and so totally immovable and utterly impractical.

My point is, you never know quite what you're going to get – some spaces are great to work in, others less so, but you can almost always make some changes for the better.

Look at how the children – and your fellow staff, for that matter – negotiate around the space. Are there any bottle-necks? Where are the desire lines?

I love the concept of desire lines; it can be really useful at school – inside and in the playground. It's a planner's term for where people really *want* to go, rather than where the actual paths are. We've all seen those forced gaps in the car park flower beds outside the supermarket, where people have chosen to take the shortest route regardless of the obstacle, and just barged their way through until it becomes the new path. Those are desire lines, and some young children are particularly prone to moving as-the-crow-flies, sending chairs and whatever else flying!

It's also worth considering that you may have children with special requirements come to join you at some point – could you accommodate wheelchair users without fuss, for example?

In theatre and television, once the cast has read the script through a few times, they have a process called 'blocking'. This involves the performers moving around the stage space to map out where the action will take place, where each line will be delivered, how exits and entrances happen, and so forth.

Having taken a good look at how everyone is moving around your classroom space, outdoor play area and any other environments they have to negotiate, have a think about whether you can make their manoeuvres any easier. Try it out for yourself – block it through. It's also worth reminding yourself that your children's view of the space is very different from yours. Check out what is level with their eye-line and how much they have to crick their necks to look up in order to access important information or equipment. I have seen some classes with display areas at child's height, so that they are able to arrange displays themselves. Having extra responsibility for their environment often leads to them having greater respect for it.

You may find yourself in a room without much scope for change, but there are still little tricks you can employ. We all know that to a certain degree, children need stability and consistency – it's not going to help anyone if the position of the coat-hooks is constantly changing, for example. However, once your children have become used to the status quo, to the daily routine, once they have come to expect the norm, it can be really useful to shake things up a bit. If you are always facing the whiteboard at the start of the day, why not face the window for a change? Or take the register in a completely different place from usual? These small changes in surroundings or routine can give a fresh focus, a new outlook, and can help gain increased levels of attention. Of course there are some children for whom this would be too upsetting, and for whom it would have the opposite of the desired effect, especially those on the autistic spectrum. You have to use your professional judgement. But just remember that your space is exactly that – *your* space, *your team's* space and it can be as useful a tool as other more obvious ones at your disposal.

As well as piquing interest and utilising the unexpected, you can use your space to manage expectations. It can be as simple as moving all the tables to the edge of the room, screening off a particular area, putting cloths over benches, introducing a new object such as a large cardboard box. 'What's going to happen today?'

Theatre has been using these kinds of tricks for decades. We are mostly familiar with the traditional set-up – we go into the foyer or the bar, then we are called by the bell and we enter the auditorium and sit facing the stage. If we are led from the foyer onto the stage itself, say, for a performance that is going to happen all around us, our expectations are heightened, there is additional anticipation, and our sensory awareness is put on alert.

One of my favourite things about young children is the reliability of their behaviour when you put them in a large space such as the hall, or even when you just move the tables back. There may be one or two who will feel a little intimidated and cling to a grown-up or huddle near the edge but, by and large, they will run. They will run back and forth, all over the place, into each other, and then that will usually coalesce into running round and round in circles, with some brave souls sliding on their knees and bottoms if the surface allows it.

Over the years, I have come to the conclusion that it's best to let them do this for a bit, to get it out of their systems and then they are much more likely to concentrate. One little four-year-old girl overheard me muttering to myself, 'Why is it that they always do that?' as I watched a dozen or more of her class hurtling round and round the hall at top speed, laughing their heads off. As she whizzed by me waving her arms in the air, she shouted out, 'It's because we need to!'

And as we've already discussed – she's right.

However, you also need to be able to rein in that energy. Some people will allocate coloured dots or similar, one for each child to stand on, to try to bring a bit of order. I'm not a fan of that. I think it is too stifling psychologically and it gives a strange message of 'yes, be physical – but not too much'. There's also an homogenising effect in having everyone be allocated their own identical little place from which they may not move. I think if you're going to be physical – be physical!

Early on in life, we are trained to associate different areas with different activities: where we eat, where we sleep, where we bathe, more often than not are separate rooms. This carries on into our work-lives, whether it's dressing room, make-up room and shooting stage; open plan office, meeting rooms and canteen; or consulting room, scrub-up area and operating theatre. So I use the same system when holding movement sessions in large spaces.

What I tend to do is to place myself on a large mat, or collection of mats depending on the size of the class, and I have a signal for everyone to come and join me there when it's time for the next instruction. I like to give these instructions in as conspiratorial way as possible. That is, we get down low and huddle together, I speak in little more than a whisper and as if I am giving them a secret magic spell. This means that they have to be quiet (although there's generally a lot of huffing and puffing!), focus, and listen to me. They also have to bring their energy down, which is often a bit of a relief for them – it's easy to forget that children get tired too. Then there's the signal for them to go back out into the space, raise the energy again and complete the task they have been given.

Variations of this can also work in your classroom, but if you don't have that much space at your disposal, there are ways that you can introduce a bit of movement to help disperse that physical energy.

~~~~~~~~~~

Most of us utilise carpet time or something similar as part of our school day. It's convenient for taking the register, sorting out lunch arrangements and sharing important information. It also helps build that feeling of team, a sense of community, and it is the perfect set-up for storytelling, for sharing, and for delivering some areas of the curriculum.

At the extreme end of the scale, I have seen nursery children kept on the carpet for over an hour. No one wants that. I don't want to sit cross-legged on the floor for over an hour, so why would I expect my children to. After all, once they start to get restless, they aren't really taking anything in, so it's pointless.

On the other hand, there are times when you do need to have the class together on the carpet for extended periods of time (not for an hour though!) and when they get fidgety, you can't afford to break continuity so much that you go and do something else and then come back to the task in hand, so what do you do?

I play a game I call 'Wiggle and Still'.

It's not rocket science, it pretty much does what it says on the tin, but it does work really well.

When I see the children's concentration start to fail them and I feel I'm losing the group, I break off what I'm saying, bring my hands into the air and start to wiggle my fingers, wiggle my head, wiggle my bottom, whilst saying: (surprise!)

Wiggle Wiggle Wiggle
Wiggle Wiggle Wiggle
Wiggle Wiggle Wiggle
and STILL.

The children are allowed to wiggle along with me, but on the 'STILL', they must freeze.

The wiggles can last as long as you wish, and be as fast or as slow as you feel like. I tend to start with long periods of wiggling and fairly short ones of stillness and gradually work it into the reverse.

The game gives them a chance to move around a little bit, but without too much disruption, and after that short break – and 'So who can remember where we were up to before the wiggle break?' – you're back on track with whatever you were doing, with a bit of renewed focus.

~~~~~~~~~~

Allowing for children's innate physicality as part of your teaching day can pay dividends, and it doesn't always have to be a full-on break to run around in the playground. I have come across primary schools who embed physical interruptions from nursery to year six, and even some secondary schools where the children are responsible for their own physical breaks, being allowed to decide when they need to take five minutes to move their bodies in order to refresh their concentration – it's not as chaotic as you may imagine.

With little ones, you have the additional need to ensure the development of their fine and gross motor skills, so introducing more physical elements to your classes is not interrupting the learning so much as shifting it for a short while.

The introduction of silent times, where communication can only happen by gesture, can work really well. It's wonderful to see what signs your children can make up to try and make themselves understood. If you have children in your class with communication or hearing impairments who are learning to sign, then that can be incorporated into the whole class. Handled sensitively, this inclusion can help raise the confidence of that child as well the skill set of the group.

Are there day-to-day tasks that can be communicated physically as well as verbally? Are there existing signs for them that you want to use, or would you prefer to make up new ones with your children?

When you need to call the attention of your children, you may already be using a physical sign such as wiggling your fingers in the air and waiting for them all to stop what they are doing and copy you. I like to evolve that a bit with some quite complex routines, incorporating clapping patterns, changes of level, arm, leg and head gestures, and very young children are happy to give their attention and rise to the challenge of mimicking me.

Physicalising some elements of your teaching can really help embed the information in all of your children, not just the most kinaesthetic learners. Mathematics lends itself to this beautifully.

It's lovely to do this outside if the weather is fine, but it is also possible indoors. Children can represent specific numbers and order themselves accordingly; you could try colour-coding odds and evens, with PE (physical education) tabards or similar, as additional learning for the more numerically minded children. Often children find it helpful to act out, and/or see acted out, some of the basic patterns inherent in simple maths. For example, a line of five children, alternating blue and red (or just boy and girl), all the blues step forward, all the blues step back, all the reds step forward, all the reds step back and so on. The children are representing simple patterns of subtraction and addition. The brain and the body are taking in what these patterns look and feel like, so they recognise these and others like them in the future. There are plenty of maths games resources available online, and lots of them lend themselves to the adaptation of being embodied by the children, rather than using counters, for instance.

Or you can add physical rituals to the day, such as the 'Going Outside' rhyme from the previous chapter.

With routine procedures, I once again borrow from the creative process – that is, having the idea, thinking it through, talking it through, walking it through, doing it. If there are complex processes that the child has to negotiate – especially when they are new to them – it really helps to utilise this separation.

First, explain why the process (tidying up, for example) is necessary and why they have to contribute to it, then, from a stationary position, talk through the layout of the storage areas, pointing out where everything goes. Then, without actually doing the task, walk them through how it might go when they actually have to tackle it. You could get them to shadow another child whilst they tidy, by way of rehearsal. Finally they are prepared and ready to take on tidying when the big day arrives and they have to do it for themselves!

This method also works at the outset when you have a whole class of children who need to learn all the systems you wish to introduce, to ensure your time together runs as smoothly as possible.

Finally, hone your observation skills. If you carefully watch how your children move, and what their non-verbal communication cues are, they will give you a wealth of ideas of how to introduce more movement into their day. Remember that they are experiencing life with their whole bodies, all of the time, and much more than you do – but the more you can accommodate their physicality and adapt your methods to take that into account, then the stronger their learning will be.

THE KERNELS

- Children are inherently physical beings – they experience and express with their whole bodies.

- Get down to their level – see what the world is like from a child's perspective.

- Let them have a little wiggle break now and again.

Chapter 3

CAN YOU FEEL IT?

Bringing the full five senses into the daily experience by introducing activities that cover the total sensory range.

Some of my earliest work in an SEN setting was with sensory drama departments, bringing texts to life for children who were unable to engage in more neuro-typical ways. In special schools, sensory work is a key part of the curriculum, with many establishments having designated rooms filled with specialist equipment to stimulate the full sensory range of the children. It always seemed a bit of a shame to me that this focus on exploring all five senses isn't more widely employed in EYFS.

Whether introducing activities that target a specific sense, ensuring that group discussions or storytelling also involve some talk around the senses, or just taking time out to notice what we are experiencing through all of our sensory receptors, it's an area in which I've enjoyed a great many positive outcomes for the children. Here are a few ideas I've utilised in the past.

Vision

Obviously the most powerful and most heavily relied upon sense for those of us with fully functioning sight. Consequently, it's often vision that we take out of the equation when we want to concentrate on one of the other senses, and the one we leave until last when encouraging questioning through any sensory experience. However, there are aspects of our visual perception that we take for granted and there's some fun to be had with optical exercises. They are also an excellent way to strengthen children's eyes.

It can be quite hard for young children to move their eyes independently of their heads, but it's fun for them to try, and good for the muscles too. You might want to practise alone first, so you know in advance how it feels. So, keeping the head still, look up, look down, to the right, to the left and then circle the eyes in each direction. Then take both index fingers in front of you, pointing up and at arm's length, keep looking ahead and open your arms to the side until you can't see your fingers any more, then keep looking ahead and bring them back until you can just see them. Stop and wiggle all your fingers so you can see them moving without looking at them. The magic of peripheral vision! Continue to stare straight ahead keeping the arms where they are, go back to pointing both index fingers, and by just bending at the elbow, alternate touching your nose with right then left fingers, then both – now try that last one with your eyes closed, it's really easy to miss!

Finally take one finger in front of you at arm's length, stare at it with eyes wide and pull to your nose, so that you go cross-eyed – can you move each eye to look to the side and then back to your finger?

I like to get children to do the exercises facing me at first, and then in pairs, taking it in turns, looking at each other. Another good game to play individually is to ask them to stand facing a wall and, using only their eyes, write out different letters or numbers. They mustn't move their heads and should try to make the letters or numbers as big as possible. It helps if the wall is a nice neutral colour and not too vivid.

We are looking at things all the time, all day long, but a lot of the time we don't really see what's around us. Incorporating quick observation quizzes into your classes helps the children to train themselves to be more aware of their surroundings and their fellow human beings. Hold a child's hands, look into their eyes, ask them to keep looking at you and to tell you what's on the wall behind them, for example. At carpet time, ask them to close their eyes and tell you the colour of your shirt, or even your eyes – I bet you get a few peepers. You can even start leaving little prompts for them. Did anyone notice the octopus hanging from the light in the cloakroom?

Our vision is a remarkable thing, but how often do we look, but *really* look at a thing? I had a wonderful session with a nursery class where I took in some fish from the fish market, fresh that morning, so not too stinky. A great many of the children had never seen a whole fish before and, before we even started on handling them and, yes, cutting them open, the time we spent just looking at them really closely brought forth some truly excellent language work as well as developing their observational skills.

Finally, as adults, life has taught us that things are not necessarily exactly what they seem. What better way to introduce this challenging concept to our little ones than the optical illusion? There are plenty available online which you can download for free.

Hearing

I'll talk about music specifically in a later chapter, so for now, I just want to deal with the act of listening. Much like our vision, we are hearing things all the time, but very rarely take the time to stop and listen intently. An exploratory aural walk can work really well with smaller groups of children. Start at the very beginning, close your eyes and listen to the sounds in your classroom – you may want to make a list together. Then take a stroll outside (open your eyes first!); what's there? Perhaps you might be able to persuade some of the other staff to let the group into places they don't normally get to visit, for example the kitchen, the Head's office or the staffroom. Once back in the classroom there can be fruitful discussion around what they have learned about the school community, simply by listening.

Of course the sounds that your little ones will be focussed on most of the time will be the sounds of human voices, but how well can they distinguish individuals? I like to get half a dozen children up in front of the class and ask everyone else to swivel round and close their eyes. If you then ask one of the children at the front to speak – something easy that they don't have to think about remembering, like a simple nursery rhyme – can the class guess who it is? It's harder if you ask them to whisper.

If you have a large space you can also play with distance. Partnering the children up, how far away from each other can they get and still hear each other whispering? A noisier variation is to give every child a piece of paper with someone else's name on it. All they have to do is to walk around the space saying the name out loud until the child in question hears them and goes to them. The easier version is to split the class into callers and listeners, but it is possible to do it with the whole class at once. It's harder for them of course, because everyone has to both listen and call, and they can all eventually end up in one big clump!

Then there is direction to play with; talking to a person whilst you're standing behind them, or standing by their side, is very different to speaking face to face. How is it if one person is sitting and the other standing, or lying on the floor? What if everyone is standing but the person talking is sitting down? Is it possible to talk round a corner or through a screen? There are very many possibilities to explore.

Touch

It is of course easier to focus the mind on the lesser senses if you take out the brutes of sound and vision that tend to barge in and over-power.

If I want children to concentrate on touch, then I like to bring in an element of mystery. One of my favourite devices is to utilise a secret bag or box that contains…who knows what? The only way to access the mystery object(s) is through a hole only large enough for one little hand. One of the things that I really like about this activity is that even though you will undoubtedly be with a group of children, and only one at a time can have a feel, the other children are always really fascinated and focussed on the reaction of the child whose turn it is. You can concentrate on extremes of texture, such as fluffy, smooth or rough, and encourage their descriptive powers, or else ask them to identify exactly what that object is, using only the sense of touch. Quite often, the very act of putting your hand into the unknown is challenge enough, without even feeling around too much, and of course some children will be braver than others. If you are able, it's quite fun to have two bags on the go with highly contrasting contents for an added element of surprise.

A different element of surprise is used in what I call The Feather Game, which is a summer game really, as you need to have a fair amount of exposed skin to make it work. This can be played by pairs of children, but it's best to demonstrate 'grown-up on child' to start with. The child lies on the floor with their eyes closed, or blindfolded; the grown-up has a feather. All that happens is that you gently touch the child with the feather, then pull it away and wait, then do it again in a different place. What is strange is that our brains can't help but make a prediction as to where the feather will touch, and that prediction is almost always wrong.

There are other ways in which our brains are confused by the sensations we experience through our skin.

Take three bowls of water, one hot, one cold, one tepid, and place them in a row with the tepid one in the centre. If you then put one hand in the hot, one hand in the cold, hold them there for a couple of minutes and then put both in the central tepid bowl, each hand will feel the water at a different temperature – like magic!

Smell

We forget about smell really, until something noxious leaps up and repulses us (always possible in EYFS!) or something fragrant enchants us. We very rarely use it deliberately.

I have come across teachers who will actively use aromatherapy in their classrooms, burning lavender oil when they want to bring the energy down and calm the children, rosemary when they want to heighten concentration, and jasmine to enhance mood. I must confess that it's not something I have personal experience of, but I see no reason not to experiment – and at least it makes the room smell nice! I have, however, used lavender oil to calm on a more intimate level; a few drops on a comfort blanket or handkerchief for a particularly distressed individual, or to aid sleep, does seem to work wonders.

More than this, it's important to alert our children to the joys of smell, to help them pay attention to this oft-overlooked sense. When holding a group discussion around the story you're telling, don't forget to ask about the smells; it's a powerful way to help develop imagination. Some books are brilliant for this, especially those that deal with food, different environments (e.g. seaside then forest) or particularly stinky characters – there are even those that reference that all-time crowd pleaser, poo.

Almost every book has something that you can enhance with a little sensory embellishment, and the children can help bring it all together too. If you're using a story to inspire your role-play area (see next chapter) then endeavour to include stimulus for each of the five senses, including the olfactory ones.

And of course you can take the most direct route and introduce the children to the actual source of some distinctive smells – we're back with fish in the classroom again! There is the old parlour game of having a blindfolded contestant guess the objects on a tray merely by smell. Some of my favourites (apart from fish) are: onions, smelly cheese, lavender, lemon, orange, coffee, mint, pine needles, vinegar, and grass.

Or you can be more mysterious and use a collection of darkened, unmarked bottles containing different scented oils – or similarly anonymous boxes if you're using dry goods – either as another guessing game, or to be passed round as stimulation for analytical discussion, and descriptive language development.

Taste

Obviously smell and taste are very much linked through our whole olfactory system, and it can be difficult, even for adults, to be absolutely certain whether we are experiencing a sensation as a smell or a taste.

Consequently, it can be worthwhile combining the two in your sensory explorations. For example, if you play the objects-on-a-tray game with edible components, the contestant may be allowed to taste if they have failed to guess just by smelling.

Mostly, though, it will be cooking that allows you to explore the wonders of edible tastes and textures.

In terms of highlighting the sensory experiences of food, I really enjoy getting other adults involved. When working in a school that has been attended by children from many different cultures, I've always found parents or other family members very keen to come in and share what may be new culinary experiences for some of the other children. And of course they have the expertise to know what dishes the children may be able to turn their hands to themselves. In more mono-cultural settings there are, nevertheless, usually local families that you may be able to coerce into a special school visit.

If that isn't your cup of tea, you can scale down and still have impact. I can remember the first time my father brought home a pomegranate, like a miraculous jewel it was, and older generations have similar memories of their first banana. Today it's relatively easy for us to find exotic foodstuffs, which, whilst they might be day-to-day for some of your children, may be unfamiliar to others. What's the strangest taste sensation you can find to share? And after all, you can always ask the children – what are their favourites, what is the strangest or strongest thing they've ever eaten, is there anything they've always really wanted to taste but haven't?

In a similar way to how you increase impact of learning by covering visual, auditory and kinaesthetic modes, when you put all five senses together you mix a powerful brew. One of my well-used activities is a 'sensory journey'. This can work with the children sitting or lying on the floor, or seated at tables resting heads on arms. First, choose your category: it needs to be something simple that they can call to mind, perhaps a favourite place, their holiday, a special day or even a dream for the future. Whatever you choose, stress that it should be a *happy* memory. Give them enough time to think of something, then ask them to close their eyes. Then work your way through the senses as you guide their visualisation, giving enough time for them to think between prompts. Is there anything they can taste or smell? Can they feel anything on their skin? Are they indoors or outdoors? What does the air feel like? What are they wearing? What position are they in? What can they feel through their feet, or the rest of their body? Can they hear any sounds? Any voices? If so what are they saying? And, finally, what can they see? All they need to do is listen and think; they don't need to verbally respond to your questions. For younger children, though, it can be helpful to start the activity by working through a shared memory together –

something that they have all experienced together in school – verbalising the different elements as a group. This helps them get used to the process before they explore their own personal memory in silence.

Once they are there, fully remembering, give them a few minutes to enjoy it, then tell them you are going to count to three, and when you get to three, you are going to ask them to blow out some air and open their eyes. One, two, three!

Although simple, this is in some ways quite a sophisticated exercise; some children will really warm to it, and others might not. However, I have always had fascinating discussions after conducting it, with children being enthusiastic to share and their descriptive language often surprising me with its intricacy.

This intimate personal activity, which requires no props or physical interaction, lies at one end of the scale, but every now and again, it's really worth pushing the boat out and going BIG!

~~~~~~~~~

Having had so much success with the exploration of actual fish in the school I mentioned earlier, the team and I decided to focus on the seaside to engage the children, taking over the school hall for a couple of days for a full-on immersive experience at the beginning of the summer term.

One of the artists I was working with lived by the coast, so she collected buckets of seaweed, crab carapaces, sponges, shells, shingle, pebbles and other flotsam and jetsam. She also bought in actual sand and seawater for the children to smell and taste. We were in the Midlands, and some of the children had never been to the beach. We collated any materials and paints we could find that were blue, green or white and used some polystyrene beads for spume. Arts supplies such as willow withies (decorative strips of willow), bubble wrap, card, newspaper, glue, tissue and so forth were provided for the children to create sea creatures, and we even got hold of several sets of goggles, snorkels and flippers, rubber rings and two inflatable boats.

The hall was zoned off into three areas; one for the children to make their sea creatures; one with all the gym mats laid out to form a large blue area for the children to create a water world that they could then swim in, sail on, and generally generate aquatic movement; and we covered the third area in many layers of brown paper so that they could paint and create a seascape of their own.

They made fish, starfish, a child-sized shark out of papier mâché, and a truly enormous octopus that took three people to carry. The paint for the seascape was in buckets and applied with mops, then they added various bits of cloth, the spume and the goodies from the real seaside. The movement activity was interesting for its shifting perspective – where did the waves have to move to for being on the water, in the water and under the water respectively?

We played a soundtrack of waves, seagulls and other coastal and marine noises. The smell of the seaside was in the air throughout, from all the foraged bits and pieces, and we even had fish pie and ice cream (not together) for lunch.

Everything was filmed and photographed, and when we had our end-of-term sharing for parents and other guests, the children were more excited about recounting this experience than any other event that had taken place in the intervening weeks.

It gave us a great kick start to the half-term, with a real wow factor, but also acted as inspiration for a whole bunch of curriculum delivery – from literacy and maths to PSE (Personal, Social and Emotional development), understanding the world, expressive art and design, physical development and obviously communication and language. In fact I would say that the thing that sticks in my memory most about this project is how well the children worked in collaboration. There was a lot going on, but they shared, they took turns, they made compromises, and they explained themselves, their desires and intentions to each other and to us clearly and thoroughly. I can remember only one brief squabble – which over two days in such a stimulating environment seems like a bit of a miracle.

~~~~~~~~~~

So I'll finish this chapter where I started, in sensory drama. That work really inspired me, and showed me how much could be gained by bringing sensory elements to storytelling. You don't need to have a great deal of money either. I have used prunings from my garden for forests or long swishy grass; a combination of ice cubes, fans and shredded paper from a local office block for snowstorms; sound effects downloaded from the internet for free; and stinky cheese – not necessarily cheap but you don't need much! Or try dried leaves and twigs for crunchy autumnal effects; latex gloves filled with jelly; seaweed, crab shells and those inevitable fish!

THE KERNELS

- Encourage sensory exploration and incorporate all five senses – sometimes go small, and sometimes risk going big!

- Use storybooks as stimulus for discussions around the senses.

- If you want to focus on another sense, limit visual input.

Chapter 4

REAL ROLE PLAY

Making role play in the classroom an effective tool for learning, whether in specified areas, in broader contexts, or in more practitioner-involved ways.

Different schools utilise role play in different ways, but I don't think I've ever worked in a nursery or reception setting that didn't include it in some way.

The least successful methodologies I have witnessed have been when a certain area of the room is set aside as the role-play space, the theme is decided by the teacher every half-term (usually on the same rotation each year) and some cloth and a few relevant props and bits of costume have been put in the corner to remain, undeveloped or added to, for the duration. It's a bit tick-box. I'm not saying that you have to create an amazing theatrical extravaganza, but I am saying that it needs to be thought about, whatever way you decide to tackle it.

The first question to ask yourself is what do you want the children to get from their role play? If you decide that you want them to develop focus then you might want to limit the range of what they have at their disposal – rabbit ears and tubes, for instance. If, on the other hand, you want them to work on decision making and co-operation, then it makes sense to give them a subject with the potential for lots of alternative stimuli, such as 'jobs people do'. Or if it's their creativity and self-expression you want to encourage, then you could give them something quite minimalist and open, maybe black paper on the walls, silver pens, silver foil, silver card and safe scissors, so that they can create their own night-time sky environment. One school I know opted for a huge gauze cube (each side around five foot long) with pockets and places to hang things – you could see through it, but once inside it felt very cosy and secure, and it allowed the children to adapt the space to whatever imaginative journey they felt like going on that day.

Then there's the structure of your role play to consider. Do you have an identified area, and if so, how long will you keep one theme in place? Alternatively, or if your room doesn't have space for that, perhaps a designated time for role play is a viable option. Some people like to hold a big event, such as Arctic Week, and still others embed role play into their regular choices for the children.

There isn't a right or a wrong way, it just needs to be thought about. In the past I have heard, 'We just don't have time!' But with a bit of planning and forethought you can set up something that will last for several weeks, that requires little maintenance and which continues to inspire your children.

In my experience, role play works best if the children are involved right from the beginning – especially if you are going to have a specific role-play area. Decide with the group (your team, remember!) what the role-play theme should be. In offering up your suggestions, cover choices based on different people, places, narratives – even try more abstract concepts such as bright, soft or hot. Yes, there will probably be some divide, and sadly it is still often along stereotypical gender lines, but it's a good learning process for the children, and you can always remind them that it can be changed further down the line. Once your theme is decided, make a proper plan together, talk about how it should look, maybe even design and draw it out on paper. You could have examples at the ready to help them along, but do watch out for their desire to just copy whatever you suggest!

If the children are able to contribute to the space, they are more likely to treat it with the level of respect that you're aiming for. I remember a beautiful tree made by the children in one reception class. Everyone painted bits of paper brown for the bark and stuck them onto the basic wire structure. The whole class made leaves to stick to the top and gradually, woodland creatures and birds were added, whether handmade or toys brought in. For a whole term the children were various woodland creatures and elves and fairies that lived in the trunk around the roots, as well as birds that nested in the branches – it was gorgeous. Not terribly robust, in truth, but it lasted because they thought of it as theirs and they wanted it to stay functioning and available for them to play in.

As I recall, it was a parent who came in and helped construct the basic framework of the tree, and this kind of project can be a brilliant way to get parents involved in school.

~~~~~~~~~~

I worked in an infant school where the nursery and reception classes shared a play space out back. Some tarmac, some grass with an unsightly metal strut fence separating them from the local park. It looked ugly, and felt a little exposed. Consequently not much play happened on the grass near the fence, with children mostly occupying themselves on the tarmac area next to the classrooms.

Quite a few of the children had expressed interest in transport, especially in trains – so we hatched a plan.

It started with an idea rooted in making more of the outdoor space, and ended up being the theme upon which the whole curriculum delivery hung for one half-term. We decided to paint a train, on panels and hang it on the fence. Father's Day was a few weeks away, so we planned a launch event, inviting dads and grandads in particular to come and help us hang the finished panels and celebrate completion.

As a starting point and inspiration for the project, we took the children to the local station (about 15 minutes' walk away, which they managed beautifully both there and back) and on a short train ride. As we had consulted with the rail staff in advance, they were super helpful and were happy to hang out with the children, giving information and answering questions. The class were so excited and so interested, with the ones who had prior experience pouring out their expert knowledge to the newbies. The visit had a much greater impact than anyone had anticipated and really consolidated their independent learning around a theme.

Over the following weeks, the children helped design the train, choosing colours and so forth, and a great deal of maths was involved in the process. Literacy came into play with writing the invitations to the launch, and arts and design was inherent, as were the three prime areas. Everyone joined in the painting of the train and when the big day came, children made snacks, sang train songs and showed their parents what they had learned about railways and rail travel.

After the event, we left a box of costumes and props outside by the train and it became an ongoing role-play area. What we noticed was how beneficial the visit had been to them in their imaginative play; having that real-life experience to feed into their role play really enhanced the quality of it.

~~~~~~~~~~~~~

Although the outside role-play area remained, the train theme throughout lasted a little over one half-term and, to be honest, when we looked back, that was perhaps a little too long. Some themes will sustain longer than others and I think rather than try to shoehorn something that needs more time into a too-short period, or conversely eking it out for longer than is appropriate, just let each theme be as long as it needs. You develop an eye for when the children are over it, it's run its course and it's time to move on.

As I've said, there are many ways to handle role play. You may choose to go the route of a big event, for a day, a week, or even longer. Or you may be part of a school that opts for a major project that involves everyone in the school community. I've heard of pupils coming in on a Monday to find that a space-ship has crash landed in their playground! Even on a smaller scale, you don't have to be confined to a single area. I had a lovely project that ran for one afternoon a week for a half-term, around the mystery of Red Riding Hood. It was a sort of 'Crime Scene Investigation: Red Riding Hood'! We started in the forest school area. I had given them no hints but had left clues for them to find, to enable them to guess the story we were dealing with. They pieced together the clues, guessed the theme, and over the weeks we put together what we thought might have happened – not necessarily following the traditional narrative. We role played interviews with Red Riding Hood, the Wolf and Grandma; drew maps and collated evidence; wrote our theories and presented them to the rest of the class. Red Riding Hood was found guilty of lying!

The children directed and did all the work themselves, I acted merely as Chief Inspector, okaying or refusing permission for plans, guiding them and helping them bring their imagined investigations to fruition. Of course it's not always necessary – or even desirable – for you to join in, but if you do choose to, make sure you have a very clear role too.

Most schools have story days, or celebrate World Book Day by dressing up. It's always the staff who don't really join in who end up looking a bit wrong. The children love it so much and it's an opportunity for you to display your sense of fun – to show your commitment to them in a playful way. I do hope you have occasions where you too can indulge in a bit of role play and really enter into the spirit of things. Your children will love you for it, and will therefore want to please and to learn from you more.

One wonderful reception class I worked with created a fantastic project around The Gingerbread Man. The children got one of the teachers to lie down on some tough card and they drew around her. Then with the application of rusty coloured cloth, paper, paint and tissue, they transformed this outline into a gigantic gingerbread man. They then used this massive puppet to play out the story, with all the children joining in. The re-enactment got a bit boisterous, but there was plenty of problem solving and co-operation in there.

This is all a tremendous amount of fun, but we also have to knuckle down and ask ourselves how we capture what the children get up to in role play, especially if it's undirected. How do we assess what's going on for them and what they are learning? We also need to ask ourselves how, if at all, this kind of play differs from what they get up to in the playground? What does it mean to them? Don't be afraid to instigate some deeper conversations with your children around these issues, but as well as words, I find visual capturing very useful – and that's the next chapter…

THE KERNELS

- Know your purpose – what do you want your role play to achieve?

- Let your children be involved in the decision-making process right from the beginning.

- Consider a visit to kick-start the project, and invite parents to participate, either in making or for a special event.

Chapter 5

LET ME SEE

How film and photography can be used as creative tools to embed learning and develop self-awareness.

I know that it can be difficult fitting in everything that you want or need to do in a day or half day, and it can be hard to stay on top of the requirements for constant assessment unless you get a robust system in place.

For myself, it's mostly been a case of just getting into the habit, getting into a routine of collecting and collating evidence so that it doesn't pile up and become a massive chore. Also, you know what it's like, something wonderful happens for a particular child, and you may be lucky enough to get it on camera, but unless those photos are dealt with fairly soon, the moment will be forgotten and it'll be buried in the hurly-burly of the week.

When I'm working, I try to keep a camera with me at all times and, more importantly, to remember to take photos as often as I can. I also have a notebook to scribble in, so that at the end of the day, I can download the photographs, get rid of the unimportant ones and cross-reference the useful ones with my notes.

Once again, the crucial thing is to know *why* you are collecting this information. It's usually as a record of your children's learning, to be shared with your colleagues, with management and with parents, but it can also be used as a tool *for* your children's learning.

There's something intriguing about discussing photographs with children. It seems that the one level of removal not only fascinates them more than discussing an event as it happens in real life, but it also helps them to make observations and analyse. It's more than just having time to study that frozen moment – although that helps of course – and it can be very useful for getting across less tangible concepts.

Most schools have a set of values or behaviours that they hold as key and want to instil in their children. These generally comprise things such as perseverance, collaboration, problem solving, investigating, co-operation and so on. Photographs and videos can be very useful prompts to help children identify these behaviours. If you can show them what it looks like, they can start to recognise and replicate. There can also be value in helping children to understand their own learning by using cameras. As I mentioned in the last chapter, it can be tricky to unpick the learning in activities such as role play and free play but if you can have a conversation with the children after the event, using photographs as a prompt, it's easier for them to start to grasp what's going on, to see where their actions and interactions have been successful, where they have been less so, and why.

It can be worthwhile forming some kind of display with these photographs, so that the children can be regularly reminded of their achievements. One school I know used customised laminated pocket files, one for each child, so photographs could be kept in their file, and one photo would always be visible. These were paired with forms or notes that briefly described the child's accomplishments. It was a good way of collating evidence, especially as the whole staff were on board, and it wasn't particularly arduous. Once again, think of the height. If possible, don't have the display too high for the children to access; they will want to be able to see them properly, and some may be able to maintain their files themselves.

Other schools prefer to collate documentation into learning journals for each individual and they are a wonderful way to record a child's growth, for you, for parents and as a way to have those meaningful conversations around personal development with the children themselves. If you're not careful though, you can end up making a real rod for your own back. I have known staff to work round the clock towards the end of term to get loose bits and pieces sorted and into the journal before time runs out and the parent wants to know why their child doesn't have a thing of beauty to show them! It really needs to be integrated into daily learning in order to give the greatest benefit, and the child needs to be involved from the start as well as throughout the process. Likewise encourage all the grown-ups in your class to get into the habit of taking photographs of the children as they work and play.

When I started working in schools, if you were lucky, there were a few digital cameras knocking about for shared use – normally with a full disc and an empty battery. Then flip cameras came along, and they were cheap and really easy to use, but didn't last that long. Now, of course, we all have cameras on our phones and more and more schools have iPads or other tablets. Even though budgets continue to be squeezed, there is probably more equipment in schools with which to take photographs and video footage than ever before. Within reason, it's an activity that is accessible to all but the very youngest children – and even they might surprise you. Here's a game I invented for a nursery group:

~~~~~~~~~~

To start, we separated off a role-play area to act as a photography studio, with a white screen for the subject to stand in front of, a tripod with the camera on it and a light to illuminate the face. I started off acting as photographer, with a couple of children as lighting and styling assistants. After a short while, other helpers took over pressing the button of the camera, directing the subject, pointing lights and so forth, as one by one each child had their portrait taken. We then printed off two copies of each photo on normal A4 paper. One copy remained whole for posterity, I took the other away and, in secret, cut it into four to six pieces. The game was to hold up one piece of the portrait, to see if the children could guess who it was, just by looking at one eye, a section of hair, an ear and so forth. They were amazingly good at it, really surprising their teachers, who were not quite as adept at recognising their own class members!

The reception group next door wanted to know what was causing all the hilarity, and when they saw what was going on, they wanted to play too. The second surprise came when the nursery children said that *they* wanted to show the older kids how to do it, which, with the exception of downloading the photos to the computer and thence through the printer, they completely managed to do.

~~~~~~~~

So, if you can, do try and give your children the chance to take photographs themselves, especially if you have learning journals. The more they are involved with them, the more they have ownership of their own learning journey, then the greater the outcome will be. Even the very young children can decide what they want to photograph or what they want to include in their journals sometimes, before they're up to the task of creating their own images. Journals are also another great way of involving parents; the more you can have conversations with them about their child's specific developments, then the more likely it is that the learning will continue at home.

Using a camera also expands our awareness of the world around us; looking through that lens with a restricted view can help us to notice things that we take for granted on a day-to-day basis.

~~~~~~~~~~

Children take part in this activity either being free to take the photographs themselves, or if they are too young for that, make them a cardboard frame that they can use to show an adult the image they want you to take for them. You can go off together on a photo safari around school, or if that's impractical then the process will work equally well in your classroom.

If you frame this task carefully, the children will give you some amazing results. Ask them to look around the school (or room) for things that they don't normally notice, and that they think other people might miss too. Show them how – perhaps with that cardboard frame – if they take a photograph out of context, close up, or from an unusual angle it can be more tricky to identify what or where it is. Once the photos have been taken, you can upload them, show them to the class via your screen and see if they can guess where the images were taken. It's up to you whether you do the show and guess after each group of children return with their photographs or once everyone in the class has had a turn. If you wait until they've all done the photography part of the task, you will get a lot of repeat shots. However if you don't, it can feel somewhat bitty, and as it goes along, a stronger sense of competition arises, and it gets harder for the later groups to find something original. I tend to go with the first option, offering praise even if the photo is a repeat.

As well as sharpening the children's awareness of the world around them, it's very informative for you to see what grabs each individual's attention, and which things the class recognise.

~~~~~~~~~

It's also possible to use photography to help with emotional communication. In EYFS, in SEN – especially with children with EBD (emotional and behavioural difficulties) – and with those whose first language is not English, I have used home-made emojis to help them be able to express their feelings. Sometimes it's easier for them to show what's going on than it is to find the words to explain.

I've mostly focussed on photography here, but many of the same principles apply to the use of video. Children love to see themselves, and other children, up on screen, and it's a marvellous way to draw their attention to what you are seeing in them. This is particularly useful in confidence building; if they can see themselves doing something they can be proud of, something that you value too, then they just have to admit their worth to themselves.

You don't even necessarily need to make recordings to make use of video. If you want to demonstrate or draw attention to something small scale and intricate, you can use your camera's zoom function and play it directly onto your screen so that the children can see it enlarged.

There is a later chapter to help you with dance and movement sessions, but it's worth mentioning here that you can achieve really positive results using a live feed in order to project the children directly onto a screen as they move. It's fascinating to see them working out cause and effect through the movement itself, exploring distance and perspective, and their relationship to each other. There might be a mad scramble to get closest to the camera, which you can manage by holding it high above their heads, or by shifting the focus to something else – a change of music perhaps.

In this day and age, children are a lot more used to being filmed or photographed than they used to be. When I first worked in children's television we used to test material by sitting the children in front of the TV and showing it to them whilst filming them with a digital camera discreetly positioned on top of the set, careful not to draw their attention to the fact that they were being filmed. Nowadays you can pretty much shove a camera right in their faces (not that I would of course!) and they're positively blasé about it.

So much of our lives are recorded and shared, it's no longer the extraordinary experience it once was to see ourselves looking back at us. But for little ones, there is still a fascination with the images themselves, and with creating them. They will see parents and siblings recording life on a day-to-day basis, and they will undoubtedly want to have a go themselves from an ever earlier age. Cameras are everywhere, so there's really no reason not to hone your skills in using this highly valuable and flexible tool.

THE KERNELS

• Get everyone involved with collecting photo evidence.

• Wherever possible, allow the children to take photographs themselves.

• Discuss photographs or video with your children – help them feel proud of their achievements.

Chapter 6

BRING THE NOISE!

Using music and vocalisation, not only as isolated events, but to assist learning throughout the day.

Sound is a powerful tool, but also a subtle one. In theatre, film and television you rarely notice it when it's right – it usually only stands out when something is wrong. Many of us have experienced not being able to hear what's going on properly or being deafened by an overly loud soundtrack; it's frustrating. And it says a lot about how important our aural sense is to us that radio is still such a popular medium. Even those with hearing impairments use the vibrations of sound to support the visual information they receive.

The quality of our spoken voices is a crucial factor in our communications, but unless we depend on it to make a living, as an actor or singer, say, how often do we think about it? Yet teachers *do* rely on their voices at work. Again, we probably don't think about it until it goes wrong, until we have a sore throat from an illness, or from spending all day shouting and trying to be heard. We tend to trust in our instincts as to when we need to raise or lower our voices, and very few of us would ever think to warm up our voices; however, a bit of forethought and a few simple exercises could really help us.

Let's start with the breath. In a quiet, private moment, just close your eyes and think about how you breathe. Don't try to change it or do anything, just breathe naturally and notice where it happens. Do you naturally have your mouth closed or your lips slightly apart? Where do you feel the movement and how much movement is there? Do you feel that your breath happens high up in your body or low down? Is it shallow or deep? Most of us breathe quite shallowly, up high in our ribcage.

Now really try to use your stomach as you breathe, pushing it out as you take a breath in and drawing the belly button back towards the spine, sucking the stomach in, as you exhale. You might want to place your fingertips over the inverted V at the base of your ribcage, where your diaphragm is, to try and feel how that muscle helps the stomach move in and out as it regulates your breath. This is one way of breathing – your diaphragmatic breath.

Now relax the stomach and take your attention to the ribs. Try to expand the ribcage as much as possible on your inhalation, as low down as you can, and particularly concentrate on the side and back of the ribs. Don't let your shoulders lift or your throat tense up. You may like to wrap your hands around the side of your ribs, so you can push against them as you breathe in. When you exhale, breathe out as much air as you can and feel that inverted V at the front of the ribcage narrow. This is a second way of breathing – your intercostal breath. (Your intercostals are the muscles between your ribs.)

You can now try and combine the two. All this deep breathing might make you feel a bit light-headed, so sit down – and have a glass of water if you need to.

It should help you realise how little of your breath potential you tend to use, and this is enhanced if you add sound.

Go back to your normal breath, and on a regular exhalation hum out a note. Now try it with the stomach breath, then the ribcage breath, then the combined breath.

You are likely to find that your note not only gets longer, but also stronger and more sustained with the last three in comparison with the first. Which exactly is the most powerful will depend on your specific musculature and habit, and the more you practise, then the better all three will get.

This is not only good for when you want to produce a nice steady loud voice for any sustained amount of time, but will also give you some extra oxygen to enliven your whole system.

Whilst I haven't used that detailed a breathing exercise with the children themselves, I have used a more simplistic version and it's worked reasonably well. In case of dizziness, I prefer to have the class lying on their backs. Also they can then feel the back of the ribcage pushing into the floor, and you can even put a cushion, a small beanbag or a toy on their tummies to help them feel the stomach pushing in and out. Another variation is to put a three-inch or so length of straw in the mouth (this one is better sitting or standing) and hold the palm of hand a little way from the end of the straw. Take a nice deep breath down into the belly, and then try to sustain a steady stream of air onto the hand for as long as possible.

Now let's think about the mouth – and these vocal exercises are really fun to do with the children, as well as being beneficial for all. I know vocal warm-ups have a reputation for being a bit silly, even among actors, but with small children that's really not an issue, is it? More of a benefit!

~~~~~~~~~~

First, as an extension of your breathing and to exercise the diaphragm further, put your mouth in the shape to make a 'Fffff' sound, then make that sound in a series of bursts, that is in a short, strong staccato way. Now put your fingertips onto your diaphragm (just below that inverted V of the ribcage) and see if you can make those little explosive 'Fffff' sounds by sharp contractions of the diaphragm.

For the facial muscles, stretch your mouth as wide as possible and then close it again whilst whispering a 'Mwwawwwm' sound. After a few of those, stretch your eyes super wide, as well as your mouth, and stick your tongue out then scrunch your features up as small as possible, and repeat half a dozen or so times.

Then for the lips, as quickly as you can, repeat the following sounds 16 times:

Mah (the 'a' sound is short as in cat)

Dah

MahDah

Puh (the 'uh' sound as in under)

Duh

Buh

PuhDuh

BuhDuh

Then make a series of the fastest little air kisses that you can, and blow some big floppy raspberries – very funny!

Now take a deep breath, and sounding out a single note, go through all the vowels 'aaaaaeeeeeeeiiiiiioooooooouuuuuuu', and try it in reverse.

To finish off, go for a good old fashioned set of musical scales, from low to high and back again.

Now you and your voice(s) are ready for anything!

~~~~~~~~~~

We all have different levels of confidence when it comes to vocalising or singing. It can feel quite exposing if you're not used to it, but as in all things, your attitude can be catching. So the more you increase your confidence in your own voice, the more your children will feel confident in theirs. It's comforting, I think, to reassure the children that you are not ever going to force anyone to sing on their own. There may be those who will want to, but it's good to alleviate any stress for the shyer ones.

Singing is a wonderful thing for you to play with in the classroom. As a variant to just saying your instructions, singing them out for a change can really help the children to take notice, amongst all the other bits of information they are absorbing at any given time. Similarly if you need to get their attention, or need them to quiet down, singing that call to attention can really cut through the noise. 'Everybody look this waaaaay… Thank you very muuuch!' You may like to make up some little songs with the children to herald different regular events or jobs that need doing, or simply to sing out 'Good afternoon' and the taking of the register. With one group of children in an SEN setting, we invented tunes for everyone's name, so that they had a musical signature as well as a regular name.

As well as the traditional three Rs, the triumvirate of Rhyme, Rhythm and Repetition are your true friends in EYFS – I could add another couple too, Ritual and Routine. I've talked about the importance of ritual in an earlier chapter. Your routine will run more smoothly with the inclusion of ritual, and your rituals will be more successful if you can employ rhyme, rhythm and repetition. I am particularly fond of a call and response structure. It demands input from the children, they need to pay attention, and they have a responsibility to make a contribution to the process. When people feel part of an operation, they are more likely to commit to it. If I may digress for a moment, there's a great story that illustrates this point. When the first manufacturers of cake mix introduced their product to the market, they were disappointed to find that it didn't sell.

They couldn't understand why the housewife didn't want to buy a mix to which she only had to add water and bake in order to produce a cake. Their subsequent research showed them that the women felt too far removed from the process, that they didn't feel as if *they* were making the cake. So the manufacturers kept the product exactly the same, but changed the instructions, stating that an egg needed to be added – and it worked. The egg was completely unnecessary, but it made the housewives feel that they had a part to play in the construction of the cake. So – when you want buy-in from your children, always remember to give them the opportunity to add that metaphorical egg!

Music is a very potent force for children; the longevity of nursery and playground rhymes attest to that. Incidentally, the most popular nursery rhyme by some margin is 'Twinkle Twinkle Little Star', followed by 'Baa Baa Black Sheep', which uses almost identical musical intervals. If you want to use an existing tune to put new instructional lyrics to, I would suggest using one of these. It's a method that seems to work especially well for tidying up time, and for lining up to go anywhere. Don't underestimate the effect music can have on mood either; it pays to have a good collection of tunes that you can draw on to influence how the children feel, and therefore how they behave.

The other side of all that noise making is, of course, listening. If you are making music with your children, with voices, drumming or even with instruments, it's a good idea to stress that in order to make good music, everyone has to be really, really together – and that the best way to be really, really together is to really, really listen. Listening is the most important thing. We don't need to talk when we're making music – we need to listen. The musicians that I have worked with in schools always take full advantage of being able to play the conductor's role. In particular, use the 'everybody stop now' signal of moving both hands towards each other in a semi-circle, and then sharply apart along a horizontal line – as if drawing two side-by-side, lying down capital D shapes. It's good to practise this sign with the children before the noise making even starts. As well as in designated music or singing sessions, you can use it during the vocal warm-ups, and even in other parts of the day. So every piece of music practice is really helping your children to concentrate through looking and listening carefully.

Of course there's a wealth of pre-existing music out there for you to use in class. We live in such a hectic and noisy world that it's a lovely thing to take time with your children to quietly listen to music. Just listening and then talking about how the music makes them feel can be enough, but if you want to take it a step further, you can ask them to paint or draw, as they listen, trying to express on paper how the music affects them. Even more impactful is to bring live music into the classroom. I am not an instrumentalist myself, but have always been able to find a musician friend, or even a staff member or parent who is willing to give up a little time to come and show children their skill. The children are always intrigued, and quite often rather mesmerised to see the magical process of music being created by a human being and an inanimate object, right in front of them and at close quarters.

It's likely that the children will feel inspired to make their own music, and it's worth finding out what instruments are available in school. I can't tell you how often I've gone on a hunt and discovered a forgotten cupboard to rummage around in, finding all sorts of instruments that haven't been used for years. If you don't have that cupboard in your school, well, no matter, you can almost always find something to drum on, blocks to knock together or tins of things to shake. Making their own instruments can double the fun for your children, and double the learning. Clothing can offer up some interesting sounds too, zippers or Velcro for example, and failing that, there's the good old human body itself – full of potential for entertaining noise invention!

With today's portable technology, it's relatively simple to record your children's efforts, and they really love to have recordings played back to them. You can go one step further and create sound effects together that can then be used to enhance storytelling, or even as a starting point for story creation.

Making that move from acoustic to electric sound generation can be especially beneficial for some SEN children. Being able to get close to, or even hold, a speaker to feel the vibration allows access to the enjoyment of sound and music in a profound way.

Music is made of patterns, and the recognition and repetition of those patterns is helping to exercise the brain in ways that will be used in numeracy and mathematics, and also in linguistics. Music has its own language, wonderful onomatopoeic words that are fun to say such as 'glissando', 'diminuendo' and 'staccato'. Don't shy away from these – revel in them. Most children love a long word to get their mouths around. I have a pet theory that part of the reason that dinosaurs are so popular with little ones is their long and complex names, and the ease with which they triumphantly know their stegosaurus from their diplodocus in a way that puts most adults to shame!

So there are very many reasons to include music in your daily teaching, but it's sometimes enough to enjoy it for its own sake. The joy of music in and of itself is sufficient a reason.

THE KERNELS

- Look after your voice, and access its full potential.

- Include listening exercises for your children each week.

- Make sure to leave space in any activity for your children to add their metaphorical egg!

Chapter 7

SSSSSSH!

The power and use of non-verbal communication.

So after all that noise making, let's quieten down a little. We all know that the greatest percentage of our communication is non-verbal, and yet we very rarely deliberately use our body language in anything but the most simplistic ways. One of the things that attracted me to dance was the very direct way that performers can have a profound effect on the audience. As observers we can't help ourselves: the flinches of the crowd watching a bout of wrestling, willing the high jumper over the bar by slightly arching back, finding ourselves slumping a little further into our seats as the actress collapses in floods of tears – all these kinaesthetic responses happen subconsciously, but they do happen. Performers need to fully occupy their characters so that their physicality convinces the audience sufficiently enough to get that kinaesthetic response, but it's not a manipulation we tend to use in our day-to-day lives.

There are occasions, however, when it might be of use to be a little more aware of the signals you are giving to your children through your body. It's all very well telling an individual how disappointed you are in them, but if your body language doesn't back it up, you're not going to get taken terribly seriously. Being conscious of your own physicality is especially important when dealing with the youngest children. They are highly primed to pick up these signals, and when they are pre-language, your non-verbal communication becomes even more important. You may think that your body will naturally reflect what you are saying and what you want to communicate, but this is not necessarily the case. Once you start to take note, you might be surprised at how often you see someone telling you 'yes' whilst shaking their head from side to side as if to say 'no', and vice versa. These little unconscious signals can give you some insight into what a child is really thinking, but they can give you away to them too if you're not careful. It would drive a person insane to be continually thinking about how their every move is being interpreted, but if there's something important you need to get across, then don't forget that you can be much more effective if you ensure that your body language is in tune with your words.

With our more vulnerable children, we need to be especially aware of the messages we are giving out.

~~~~~~~~~~

I worked in an inner-city nursery with children from very many different cultures and backgrounds, some of whom had had a pretty rough ride during their short lives. One little girl had left her homeland with her mother under traumatic circumstances, had only arrived in the UK a couple of weeks previously, had no English, and was understandably nervous. I'll call her C. She was mostly occupied with just taking in all the new information, placing herself on the edge of any activity and watching in silence; in fact, C hadn't spoken at all since joining the class. At first, I tried just occasionally going and standing next to her, but she didn't like it, it was too soon for her to trust me and she always moved away. I noticed that she was very tactile and was drawn to soft, fluffy toys and objects and I had an idea. For Christmas, a friend had given me a rather strange scarf which comprised a series of fluffy blobs, spaced out every two or three inches along a central cord. The entire thing was about four feet long. I started wearing it in the playground, and making a show of stroking the end blob when I knew C was watching me. Eventually, when I thought the time was right, I took the scarf from round my neck and, whilst holding on to one end, threw the other end in C's direction. She picked it up and started stroking the soft fur. We had a connection, a link.

This was stage one, and I didn't want to rush things, so this was as far as we went for the first couple of days. Then she started to lift her gaze to look at my face, which was a first, so I decided to proceed and moved my hold on the scarf along to the next blob, bringing us ever so slightly closer to each other. C was happy with this and moved herself one blob towards me, before changing her mind and moving back again. I follow her lead and moved back myself.

Over the following weeks, C and I played this game every day. Eventually, she was happy enough to move all the way to the centre of the scarf with me so that we were standing face to face (if I bent down, that is!). Once we had broken through this barrier, the game became more about her having a way to let me know how she was feeling on any given day. If I left the scarf lying around somewhere, C would bring it to me, then with us both starting at the ends, she would move back and forth according to her level of confidence on the day.

All this took place without a single word being spoken.

Ultimately, I lost my scarf to C as she started to use it as a way to make contact with the other children in the nursery. It was a vital tool that helped her to find her place in her new community, and I couldn't have wished for anything better than seeing her laughing and playing with other children, relishing her rekindled confidence. And, yes, she did begin to speak.

The most important lesson I learned from my experience with C was to follow her lead; *she* had to dictate the pace or the whole venture would have failed. It can be difficult to resist the temptation to do something, or say something – to fill the gaps – but sometimes the best tactic is to leave that space, to not be afraid to be still and silent, to watch and wait and see what happens. No matter what form it takes, conversation is a dance, and you don't have to do all the steps yourself.

An awful lot has been written about body language, and most of us will have heard the standard chestnuts bandied about; closed positions such as crossed arms and legs will make you seem defensive and lacking in control, whereas open positions will give the impression of relaxed confidence; if you want someone to like you, move when they move; mirror a person's position to gain rapport; if they touch their nose, they're concealing a lie or exaggerating, and so forth.

I'm not saying these are untrue or not useful, but I think there needs to be a caveat, especially when you are dealing with small children – it's not always that simplistic.

Whilst the basic wisdom of closed and open positioning may hold true, some children will feel threatened if you make yourself too big. It's easy to forget how small and vulnerable they are – especially when they are so demanding – and how huge and foreboding a full grown adult can be to them. Sometimes we need to hold back a little instead of going in all guns blazing. Similarly, the mirroring or copying technique can be downright creepy if it's not handled with care and subtlety.

So for my rule of thumb, I go back to the lesson of C. A child will let you know in no uncertain terms what works for them physically and what doesn't. It's our job to hone our observation skills and take the lead from them. I like to think in terms of 'Full Body Listening', that you give your total attention in order to pick up what's going on with a child. I go into more detail on this in a later chapter but, for now, the important thing is to take your cues from the child. We all work at a different pace and with different preferences, so if you want a particular result from a particular individual, feed back what works for them and you're much more likely to succeed.

The use of a conduit has been successful for me on several occasions; the scarf in the case of C; a length of rope that one three-year-old loved to be wrapped in to help him feel safe and secure; a length of stretchy exercise band for the whole class to hold onto in a circle, to induce a feeling of unity; or making tunnels of thread together to enhance collaboration. I've played all these games almost completely non-verbally and they have all resulted in stronger bonds between those who've played them. Have a look around your place of work and see what you might have that would work as a similar stimulus for your children. Once again, watch how they are playing with each other, and see if there's anything you can develop into a broader activity, whether verbal or non-verbal.

During my time as a Teletubby, I got used to irritated parents berating me for the annoyance of having to endure the same little film of children that was shown on our tummies, twice through. I understood how this would be tedious for adults, but for the young children for whom the show was made, the thinking was sound. What we wanted to have happen was for the audience to be able to make predictions about was about to take place, which would be correct because they'd already seen it once, and this would give them a huge boost of confidence in their ability to learn. Our little ones can struggle to take in both the visual and the aural at the same time, so if you give them at least two goes at it, they are more likely to absorb the total information. It's worth bearing this in mind in your classroom, either by using repetition, or by giving sufficient time for children to take in the visual information in silence, before adding the extra layer of verbal communication, or vice versa. *Teletubbies* used this technique in many parts of the show. For example, you would always hear the oral signature of each character well in advance of seeing that character arrive, often far away. So the child could recognise the sound, make a prediction about whom they were going to see appear, their prediction would come true, and the child would feel secure and hugely empowered from making that correct prediction.

Stillness was as important an aspect of our performance as the movement, and especially stillness with eye contact straight down the lens to the child watching at home.

In a classroom situation, you can use the performer's trick of making each individual feel that you are looking at them, even though it's patently impossible for you to be looking at everyone individually at once. It's achieved by a mixture of flitting your gaze so that you briefly catch the eye of everyone in the room, and softening your gaze so that you are looking at no one in particular, but taking in the whole group. This works best when everyone is looking at you, of course, which is more likely to be the case with a theatre audience than with a group of tiny children! I like to use the clichéd Mafiosi sign of pointing two fingers to my own eyes, and one finger to the person whose attention I want. Sudden 'down the lens' eye contact is like **bold text** when applied with real intention; use the big eyes for emphasis when you need them to know you mean business.

Talking of signs, you will almost certainly find yourself in a position where you need to use some sort of visual cues in addition to, or even instead of, words. This may be as additional support for your youngest children, or for EAL (English as an Additional Language) children or for those with learning disabilities or other personal challenges presenting in your class. Of course there are existing systems, BSL (British Sign Language), ASL (American Sign Language) and Makaton being the most popular and readily available in the UK and the US. In addition, though, you may want to invent signs that are unique to your class.

It's fun for the children to create their own signs, and good for combining their imaginative and logical thought processes, whether the signs are physical gestures or drawings or both. Today's children are growing up in a world that habitually uses emojis, and we all pretty much accept that it's now the norm to express how you feel with a little symbol…or 12! That can be a useful tool for you too, especially with children who struggle to articulate their feelings. I know one little boy who, when asked to make a series of drawings showing six feelings he felt most often, drew happy, sad, confused, tired, surprised and needing a poo ;-).

On a more serious note, I encountered a selective mute for whom a combination of Makaton symbols, emojis and gestures allowed him to join in to a certain degree whilst he worked through the issues that had led to his decision not to speak.

For myself, although not proficient in BSL or ASL, I find that backing up what I say with gestures, whether I'm storytelling or giving out instructions, helps emphasise what I'm trying to communicate and lends a certain amount of weight. Some words will be easy for you to add gesture to – listen, book, small, high, hat, eat, and so on – and others will require a little more imagination – dream, sometimes, again, forever, air – but it's a job you can get the children to help out with.

That's all on the small scale. You can also have a lot of fun using non-verbal communication as part of grander projects.

~~~~~~~~~~

One Reception class was using Outer Space as its theme for a half-term. We got to talking about aliens, whether we believed in them and whether or not we thought they believed in us. We decided we'd try and communicate with them by making messages for them to see, out in the playground. The class separated into four groups and each group decided what it was they wanted to say and how they might be able to say it.

The messages were all simple things, like wanting to just make a greeting, to let them know we were here, to say that we were friendly and to invite them to visit. Knowing that the aliens would be very high up in the sky, the children realised that the messages would have to be very big – if it was just writing on paper, they wouldn't be able to see from their spaceships. It was most likely that they would fly over school in the night-time, so as the messages would have to be out in the playground all night, they would have to be made so that they wouldn't blow away or get eaten by rats! Another consideration was that we didn't know what language they would speak, so it would be most effective if we used signs and symbols. With the wonderful reasoning of children, there was a strong feeling that if the intention of making the messages was honest and true, then the aliens would be able to understand what they meant.

So, one group pinned down lengths of cloth, another used hoops and cones from the PE cupboard, the third used a selection of painted stones and branches, and the last group used pretty much anything they could get their hands on! With adult help, they mapped out how the messages would look on paper first, so that they had a plan to work from, and although there was some variation, each finished communiqué definitely bore a solid resemblance to the original plan.

They all worked vigilantly, with a tremendous sense of purpose and with relatively little squabbling.

Once everyone had decided that their messages were complete, the whole class took a tour around them so that each group could explain their project to the others. Then we all stood in one big circle around all the messages and shouted very loudly into the sky that we had something to say to the aliens, just in case any happened to be passing and we couldn't see them because it was daytime.

Then we went home.

The next day, we gathered everyone in the classroom so that we could go outside together and investigate whether or not there was any evidence that our messages had been received.

It was truly delightful to see how much the children wanted their messages to have been read. Although I couldn't really see that anything was terribly different from how we'd left it, they were forensic in their analysis:

'This branch is a bit moved – they must have poked it!'

'This cloth is blown over a bit – it must have happened with the wind when the spaceship landed.'

And so forth.

The unanimous decision was that aliens had indeed read the messages, that they had understood them, and the future of Earth was secured. A job well done. I loved listening to them talking excitedly to their parents as they went home that day: '...and they really read them. They really did.'

This simple little activity formed the basis for some really broad learning, covering the three prime areas and beyond... to space!

THE KERNELS

- Inhabit your whole body when you want to communicate something important.

- Use variance in your gaze to act like **bold text**.

- Non-verbal mirroring can encourage reluctant communicators, as long as you follow their lead.

Chapter 8

TELLING THE STORY

Improving your own storytelling techniques, as well as using each story as stimulus for other learning. Plus how to help little ones invent and construct their own stories.

The part of your job where you get to tell your children a story is probably the area most obviously linked to that of a professional performer, because for a short period of time, that's what you are. You might be aiming to give your audience something more than just pure entertainment, but nevertheless you need to keep them focussed in the same way as a stage actor does.

Naturally, we are all different and have varying strengths and weaknesses. I have worked with teachers for whom this aspect of their chosen occupation is absolutely the best bit, and others who never quite manage to shake off the feeling that they are doing it 'wrong'. It's a natural level of anxiety for those of us who might be a little shy, or who tend towards being more reserved. The good news is: there is no 'wrong'. I have yet to meet a child who didn't like having a story read to them – frankly, you can't lose. Of course, there may be certain stories that certain individuals don't enjoy so much, but you can always set up a voting system, or let everyone take a turn to choose, so that they know they will have the opportunity to select a more tolerable tale further down the line.

The key really is for YOU to be interested. Much like with acting, even though everyone is aware that you've done it before and you know what's coming next, you have to behave as if it's the very first time and every word is news to you. If it's an old favourite, and you know that they know it as well, if not better, than you, then you might think the fabrication of it being novel to you is spurious, but it's still important to deliver the words as if they are fresh.

I do appreciate that it can be a little awkward, just from a practical point of view. You want to be able to show the children the pictures, but also need to see the words yourself in order to read them out. The trick here is not to rush, take your time, you can break off from the narrative to discuss the illustration, and then carry on reading once everyone has taken in the visual information. Alternatively, technology is on hand to eliminate the problem entirely. Even if you don't have access to e-versions of books, if you find working with a screen easier, you can always scan in picture books for reading to the children. The advantage of this is that the children can *see* the words as you are reading them, so it could be argued that this enhances their literacy skills better than you reading to them from a book. The downside however is that they are looking at a screen – something they will spend a great deal of their little lives doing – and it rather takes away the personal interaction and magic of sharing the experience of being read to by another human being.

The other solution to this problem is to commit the story to memory, and with those tales that you find yourself reading over and over again, to a certain extent this will happen naturally – and it will happen even quicker if you put your mind to it a little. A word of caution though...

I was holding sensory drama sessions one day a week in a special school with a small group that included one or two boys on the autistic spectrum who could lash out when upset – as a result of how the autism manifested itself in them. We were working with Michael Rosen's *We're Going on a Bear Hunt*, and I started each session by reading the story to establish focus and remind them what we were doing. I decided I'd commit it to memory, so that I could concentrate on the children, being able to make eye contact and to observe them more closely whilst I was speaking. As you probably know, it's a simple enough story with a very clear structure, but one week I accidentally got my verses in a tangle. I told the 'thick oozy mud' and the 'big dark forest' sections the wrong way round. My mistake was pointed out to me rapidly, by one of the autistic boys launching himself at me and clamping his teeth onto my arm, managing to scream from the back of his throat whilst he hung on. I got away with nothing but a very sore bruise, he apologised to me, I apologised to him, and I was a lot more careful in the future whenever reciting a well-known and well-loved book by heart!

But, of course, what you gain by knowing at least portions of any book is that vital facial contact with your class. If you're really committed to the story and acting it out as best you can, it has so much more meaning. The lesson I have learned is that if you stumble or forget the words, nine times out of ten, one or more of the children will be able to fill in the gaps for you. In fact, I think it's desirable to leave some gaps so that they can fill in the words for themselves, then they have so much more involvement. You can really ham up this technique and totally play the idiot, asking them to explain what's going on, forgetting who various characters are and generally behaving like you are way more stupid than them. It's a game that also gives you an idea of how much they are taking in, who is and who isn't with you, and the overall level of attention.

Thus far, I've only dealt with storytelling to a group, but you may find yourself fortunate enough to have time to spend storytelling for just one or two individuals. Obviously, this is slightly different and you will adjust your performance accordingly. I think of it like a magician. It's one thing to be on a large stage executing massively spectacular illusions involving tigers and the like, and quite another to be in a more close-up setting, at a table performing intricate sleight of hand and card tricks. That more intimate situation tends to be far more personally interactive than when there are many eyes on you from a distance.

Now that you've got your warm-up exercises for face and voice down pat, you should be well equipped to add extra expression to your storytelling. Don't be afraid to be outrageous, either with face pulling or putting on silly voices; your children will engage with the story more when you can highlight the extremes for them with your performance. If you have fun, they will have fun.

If you really want to get theatrical, there's nothing to say you can't include a little dressing up, whether it's you, the children, or both. You may have stories that include characters with a defining feature, a crown for a queen for example or a wand for a magician, and you can involve the children in a more specific way by delegating these props for them to play a particular part. If you don't have the necessary items, then there's more enjoyment and learning to be had by making them.

This leads me onto the issue of getting full value out of your storybooks. There are many ways you can utilise a popular tale over and above reading it to your children. At the simplest level, you can develop their imaginations by exploring tangents to the plot and back-stories for the characters. What happened directly before this story started? What happens to these people in a year's time? When someone leaves the main narrative, what happens to them? What is that person's favourite food? What's their middle name? Do they have a pet? What are they scared of? Why? … And so on.

Then you can use the story as a starting point for other play and learning. If your story has a shop in it, for example, then that can inspire some very specific store-keeping play, incorporating some maths, communication, PSE (Personal, Social and Emotional development), understanding the world and fine motor skills – all with a particular motivation and context, which brings the activity to life much more vividly.

In my training sessions I regularly give a task where teachers work in pairs, using a picture book as inspiration for another activity. They then describe the activity, and we all have a go at it, offering up modifications where appropriate. It's something you can try yourself, and again, once you have established this as somewhat of a pattern, I'm sure your children will have suggestions of their own as to where the story can take you all next.

Then, of course, there's making up stories of your own. It's something that you get better at with practice, and I think it helps to have a framework to work within. One of my favourite ways to create a story is to have the children bring me objects. For example, they might start by giving me a toy sheep. Whatever they give first is the central character of the story, so it needs to be named – have a good look at it, and see if any personality comes through. Of course it might be something random like a pencil, so then anthropomorphise like crazy...what possible problem could a pencil have? Perhaps he (Cecil) doesn't like what he's made to draw, he wants to draw unicorns, but only ever gets to draw normal animals...he tries to put horns on everything, but they just get rubbed out...perhaps he needs to team up with the rubber? Having started, whenever you reach a hiatus, a child can bring you another object for fresh inspiration. Some journey, or task, or jeopardy is always good and if you can find something to repeat, that will act as a kind of chorus, the more the better – especially if you include sound or actions. Cecil, for instance, could repeatedly get so cross that he rolls overoveroveroveroverover and 'Plop!' Off the table. With head actions as if watching him do so.

Going back to the premise of leaving gaps for the children to fill in, you can offer them a structure to complete as you make a story up together. Here's one I've used in the past as a basic outline or starting point, and then embellished with deeper descriptions, more detailed conversation and so forth:

> There was a _____ who was going to a _____ in a _____ to see a _____.
> (S)he was called _____. On the way (s)he met a _____ and they decided to _____ together. The _____ was called _____. It was _____. They were _____. Finally they arrived at _____ and they both _____.
> _____ was _____. _____ they said, and began to _____.

Or use 'The Secret Life of Objects':

> Start to look at your surroundings in a different way. The saucepan there – does he (or she, or it, or other?!) look forward to being used, does it hurt being heated up, or does it tickle? Is a wellington boot really hoping it'll get stuck in the mud every time it goes out? Is it like a little kiss to a light switch every time you switch it on?

Take a tour around your environment to create (or discover) lives and histories and stories of the things you live with every day.

The more you can merge visual, aural and physical, then the more impact any story-based activity will have. Traditional fairytales tend to have recurring archetypes and themes; prince, princess, witch, tower, wolf, castle, forest, etc. So you can establish gestures for each of these, knowing that they will be repeated across several different stories. (You can also do this for books that are part of a series featuring the same characters.) As we all know, those traditional stories tend to start with 'Once Upon a Time' and finish with the goodies living 'Happily Ever After'. I have a standard sequence of gestures for each of these. The children love to join in, it's good for their fine motor skills – they try so hard to get that click right – and it gives a really strong indication of beginning and end. So here they are, with the explanation as to why.

Once. That's
one – one
finger held up
– one for once.

Upon. That's like on –
so there's one thing on
another – upon another.

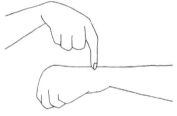

A Time. That's drawing
round the watch on your
wrist...pointing at it...

...and that's the hand of
the clock going round and
round. Tick. Tick. Tick.

And:

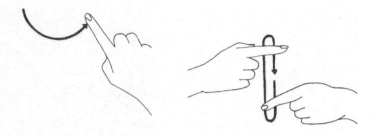

Happily. That's a big smile, a smiley face.

Ever. That's going round and round and round and never ending like a circle.

After. That's behind you, it's gone, it's over, it's after.

That's quite a small and contained way of including a physical element in your storytelling. When I want the children to stretch their imaginations to the full and get their whole body involved, something a bit more expansive is necessary. This is one of my favourite frameworks. I call it 'Wonky Dance Street'.

~~~~~~~~~~~~~

The first stage follows the format of the old parlour game 'Consequences', but on a grander scale. Put your children into groups of four or five, ideally with an adult to help each group, but that's not completely necessary. Each group is given a large and long piece of paper (lining wallpaper works well). I find it best to work on the floor, then you have plenty of room and can work with a nice big size. If you can get into some kind of hall space, then that's ideal.

Everyone in the group, except for one child, closes or hides their eyes. This is where one grown-up per group helps, to keep an eye on cheating or to distract the other children and encourage the chosen one! That one child draws a head on the paper, and then folds the paper over so that the head is hidden, leaving only two little lines to let the next drawer see where the neck is, and therefore where they need to start drawing the body.

So the next child draws the torso and arms, and then folds, leaving a clue for where the next player should begin. Then depending on the number of children in the group, the game continues with hips then legs, or hips *and* legs together, and then feet, until you are left with an entirely folded piece of paper containing a secret creature.

It's worth encouraging the children to be as ludicrous as possible. Their characters don't have to be humanoid, they can be as fantastical as they like, with whatever extra bodily accoutrements (tails, fins, whiskers, etc.) or adornments they care to include.

Once completed, if there's time, I like to go round each group and do a big reveal so that the whole class can see each group's creature. If your time is a bit limited, you can just leave each group to unfurl their artwork themselves.

Part two involves bringing life to the characters. Deciding on a name is crucial, and then I set everyone questions such as:

· Where do they live?

· What do they eat?

· What do they like to do?

· Do they have a special skill or power?

· Do they have a pet?

· What's their relationship with the other characters? (This only works with a shared reveal, of course.)

Write the answers on the paper, around the drawing.

It's not a definitive list of questions. You can add and edit as you feel, or depending on the age and personalities of the children you're working with. However, the final question is always:

· How do they move?

This is where it really helps to be in a hall, especially if you have a large group, but obviously it's possible to scale down to a smaller room if you're working with fewer children. Outside in the playground is another possibility if it's a fine day.

It's likely that more than one child per group will get up and move around, and in differing ways. Lead the discussion here, to really guide the children to look at and think about what kind of body their character has, and how it will dictate how they move. The group should be able to reach a kind of consensus, and each child to more or less display the same movement traits.

The final stage is to take the drawings, arrange them in a line with some space in between and either hang them on some bars or other equipment in the hall, on the walls, draped over chairs or such like, or even just laid out on the floor. The point is that this is where you are forming 'Wonky Dance Street'. Each group of children sits by their character. Now you need a visitor. It can be a child, it can be yourself or, best yet, another teacher who hasn't been involved in the activity thus far. The visitor is guided round to each house/den/castle/spaceship in Wonky Dance Street and introduced to each character as you read out their various attributes. When you get to '...and they move like this!' the children get up and show their wonky dance.

You might like to finish off with one big wonky dance party.

~~~~~~~~~~

It's very silly, a lot of fun, but has a great deal of embedded learning within it, as does any engagement with imaginative character and story creation, narrative structure and descriptive invention. Games like this one hit the three prime areas of EYFS as well as the support criteria, but their real value goes deeper than that.

All of our lives are dictated by the stories we tell ourselves about what's going on. What we can imagine for ourselves shapes the possibilities we feel able to explore as our lives unfurl. A limit in our ability to imagine plays out as a limitation on what we are able to envisage we are capable of – a limitation on our lives. So the more we can help our children to exercise that creative imaginative muscle, then the better prepared they will be for the unknown that is the rest of their lives. Stories help them develop emotional intelligence and critical thinking skills, whilst engendering a strengthened sense of self, as well as greater knowledge of their fellow humans and the world we all occupy.

Be aware that everything you do and say is going to be fed into each child's story of themselves. There is nothing more important.

THE KERNELS

- Be interested yourself – no matter how many times you've read a story to them, find something new and enchanting with every repetition.

- Get full value from the books you have – squeeze every last bit of provocation out of the tools you have to hand.

- Encourage your children's imaginations to run wild. Then corral them into a story.

Chapter 9

WHY PUPPETS?
HOW PUPPETS?

Just that! The purposes for including puppets, how to really use them to bring the best out of your children and some tried and tested puppet projects to implement.

I spent several years of my working life as a puppet. That's not a metaphor. I was inside a giant puppet body and head for around 11 hours a day, eight months of the year, for the best part of six years. This experience has given me some real insight into the power of puppets, and how humans react to them.

Let me illustrate with a story. Whilst we were filming, the great and the good of children's television from all around the world would be brought onto the set for the rare treat of meeting the Teletubbies. We were huge – again not a metaphor, my suit was almost eight foot from toe to aerial tip – and the only direct contact with the outside world was peering past mechanical apparatus and black netting through the relatively tiny slot that was the puppet's mouth. If I wanted to put my hands, sorry, paws, over my puppet eyes, my arms would be at full stretch above my head, so they were quite a long way from my actual eyes. The people we worked with day to day were fully aware of the reality of our situation; however, visitors tended to be completely seduced by the puppets. If, when I looked out through my mouth (!) at the puny human in front of me, I could see the upwards tilt of the chin, the stretch of the neck, then I knew they were addressing the puppet's eyes and had forgotten, or chosen to forget, about the human within. Once their voice slid into the tone and timbre that one would use to speak to a small child – quite a thing when one is actually addressing an eight-foot-tall, bright yellow, furry alien – then I knew I had them. I could pretty much say anything I wanted, as long as I stayed in character. In six years, only one visiting dignitary spoke to *my* eyes inside the costume, such was the power of the puppet, and these visitors were extremely powerful people, heads of international media companies whose specialism was communication.

So it's not just children who are susceptible to puppets; in fact, if anything, you have to be *more* vigilant with your puppeteering when your audience is very young. My TV boss insisted on very high levels of skill from all her puppeteers, so as not to fall into the anathema of 'dolly waggling'. We worked hard to live up to her expectations.

Like any form of acting, effective puppeteering is based in the dual foundation of observation and honesty. In order to recreate human actions, reactions and emotions, you need to know what they look like in other people and how they feel in yourself. A lot of this knowledge has been absorbed empirically through however long you've been alive. You don't need to think about whether your gaze tends to be lifted or lowered if you're feeling sad, you just know. However, when you are trying to breathe life into an inanimate object, it's worth having a think about some of the subtleties.

In the same way that animators will read a script in front of a mirror in order to accurately reproduce the necessary intention in their drawing or model, so puppeteers will sit in front of a mirror with their puppets, experimenting with how best to make them seem real.

I'm not necessarily suggesting that you spend hours on end doing this, but a little time spent here really does help elevate your puppeteering from mere dolly waggling to something that can have real impact in the classroom. Plus it's actually pretty good fun.

So this brings us to the purpose – why would you want to use puppets with your children, other than from a vague feeling that it's something you're supposed to do? Well, following on from the previous chapter, perhaps the most obvious use is to enhance your storytelling. There are usually a few animal puppets knocking around that you can use to bring a bit of 3D interaction to story time, and it's even more useful to have a bit of technique up your sleeve when you and the children are creating stories together.

Remember Cecil the pencil? Admittedly, it would be a bit of a challenge to breathe genuine life into him, but he's a great example of where you can employ an old puppeteers' trick. If you echo the emotion or intention that you are trying to get your puppet to convey, then your audience is likely to fill in the gaps. That is, if you want Cecil to look sad, as well as tilting him downwards, slump your own posture, lower your own head, look sadly at him and sigh. When you're using a puppet, you are creating the mood together. It's not just you manipulating the character, you need to join in too, sometimes mirroring, sometimes supporting through your relationship with the puppet, and sometimes even opposing – depending on what you want to communicate. The key is that *you* have to believe in the reality that you want your children to buy into. Each child in your class will have their own favourite toy or toys who are real to them; they are primed to embrace the fantasy you offer and to make it real.

There's a puppet framework I have used with several reception classes that has proved powerfully effective on each occasion. I'll use just one example to explain how it can go, but it's adaptable if you want to vary the structure. I've found it particularly useful in helping reception children make the transition to year one.

～～～～～～

The class had been focussing on Space as an overall theme. One day, they received an email, sent to the teacher but addressed to everyone, from a space traveller – SK417.

SK417 has crash landed on earth and is lost. He's only small, everyone looks very big and scary and he needs help.

This led to all the children writing their suggestions for a reply to SK417. Together the class decided on a response – to invite SK417 to come to the school.

The length of time that the correspondence continues can be as long or as short as feels right to keep the children interested and involved. On this occasion we eked it out for about a week, using mapping skills to help SK417 find his way to school, making welcome signs and preparing some healthy snacks as the children thought SK417 would be hungry after such a long journey.

Finally the big day arrived, and everyone was very excited. Having virtually no money for this project, we managed to find an old boy-child puppet in a cupboard, scrubbed him up and gave him some new clothes, shoes and hair...a lot of hair. The puppeteering of SK417 was based in a sense of wonder and ignorance, it gave a fabulous opportunity to ask the children myriad questions about their school, their lives and their customs, and it was fascinating to hear how they described their own experiences. Crucially, SK417 now noticed that the children had nice-sounding words they called each other, not just letters and numbers. So once they had explained the concept of 'names' the children had to decide on one for their new friend. Via a solid democratic process, Sam Hairy was born.

Sam Hairy became an integral part of the class. His presence at circle time seemed to encourage the children to communicate more freely, especially when it came to talking about themselves and their own feelings. Every week, if they wanted to, the children could write an invitation to Sam Hairy to come and stay with them for the weekend. They would then have responsibility for taking photos and writing a short piece in Sam Hairy's diary, describing what he had done, and to show it to the rest of the class on the Monday. He was a great motivator in many ways, and didn't lose his important position in the class community for the whole term.

One day, Sam Hairy went missing. There was genuine concern and the children organised themselves to carry out searches, putting up posters, making announcements in assembly and so forth.

A couple of days later, there were unprecedented levels of excitement when the wandering puppet returned. It turned out that he hadn't gone very far at all, but as he'd heard that in the Autumn the whole class, including him, was going to have to move to something called 'Year One', he wanted to go and check it out. So it was Sam Hairy (and me!) who took small groups of children to their new room, showed them round, and helped to soothe any nerves they may have had about the imminent change.

We were only a month or so into the new academic year when Sam Hairy found himself put away, back in a cupboard, no longer needed by the children. But that was fine, he'd done his job for now and, with a thorough makeover, he could be ready to resume his duties with a new identity in the summer term, when the next reception class were in need of his services.

Of course, deep down, the children knew that Sam Hairy was a puppet, but he fulfilled an important role for them that could only be effective if everyone involved bought into the game. Inevitably some children were more attached than others, and it tended to be those who were generally less verbally expressive who found the most benefit in having a conduit available to them. It wasn't unusual to have a child imbue Sam Hairy with traits or feelings that they were feeling themselves, but didn't want to admit to.

The use of puppets can be invaluable when working on PSE, and you can encourage some deeper exploration by getting the children to make their own. I've tried several different techniques in this area. On one occasion I had the good fortune to stumble across a job lot of unwanted gloves and mittens, which were perfect to use as the bases for hand puppets. Knowing that a similar stroke of luck was unlikely to happen again in the future, I also made some mitten templates in order to cut and stick together thin polyethylene foam shapes to form puppet 'blanks' for children to embellish at will to create their own characters.

If you want to get a little more obviously personal, you can draw round the children – or get them to draw round each other – so that everyone has an outline to fill. You can frame the task as the paper people being their imaginary selves, their real selves, or representative of a fictional or factual character. Once completed, it's possible to attach the paper puppets to the children, so that they are able to puppeteer their representational selves. Or, if you have space, hang them on walls or from a line suspended across the classroom.

A similar effect can be achieved through making masks – and it takes up a lot less room! Check if there is a Community Re-Use or Creative Recycling Centre near you, as it's often possible to pick up all sorts of wonderful bits and pieces for the children to use in this activity. Paper plates are a good starting point too, and pretty inexpensive, especially if you buy in bulk from the wholesalers. Just like me in my Teletubby puppet, if you go along with the pretence, you might find that once a child feels safely enough disguised behind the mask, they will reveal all sorts that they may not do ordinarily.

Once the children have become accustomed to the presence and use of puppets, you can start to get a little more ambitious. With slightly older or more able children, you can experiment with them puppeteering each other – it might be that they physically move each other around, or that a gentle tap on the back is the signal for the 'puppet' to open its mouth. Or you can encourage collaboration by getting two children to work together to operate a single puppet. Four-legged friends are best for this. For example, you can make a good shaggy dog puppet using a broom as a base, hanging legs and fur (maybe brown paper streamers) from the handle and attaching the head with wire so that it can be articulated. One child is in charge of the body, and the other moves the head (a droopy tongue and floppy ears are fun additions).

However, I still think the most value is to be had by developing a relationship with your own puppet. If you find a puppet you like, you can develop him or her or it as a kind of side-kick. Your puppet will be able to say and do things that you couldn't and, if you like, your puppet can be much stupider than you. You probably want to maintain some dignity and a semblance of authority, but your puppet is perfectly able to ask the most idiotic questions, hopefully inspiring the children to answer and have a chance to show off their knowledge. Your puppet can even take on some of your work for you. If you feel uncomfortable with dance and movement, it's a lot easier to get a puppet to perform a high kick than to complete the dance training necessary to be able to do it yourself!

Fear not, though – the next chapter is full of easy ways to get your children moving and discovering their dance mojo…

THE KERNELS

- Believe! What's real to you will be real to them.

- Pay attention to detail. The well-observed subtleties can really help bring an inanimate object to life.

- Embrace the conduit. Some children will find it easier to communicate via a puppet.

Chapter 10

GET UP AND BOOGIE

You dancin'? If not, why not? Easy ways to get your children moving, inventing physically and learning about their bodies. Also how to calm them down again afterwards!

There's no getting away from the fact that young children are hugely physical beings. They experience and express everything with all of their bodies, or with as much of their bodies that they can. You only need to look at how a toddler throws themself so completely into a tantrum to see that this is true. As grown-ups, we have been schooled in what is and isn't acceptable in polite company, but it's important for children to have opportunities to submit to the desire to physicalise – it's helping their brains grow.

As EYFS practitioners, we have a wonderful excuse to break free of the constraints of normal adulthood and join in with the wonderful world of unrestrained child movement. I know that some of us will feel less happy about this prospect than others, but I'd like to offer up a few tips, techniques and games to make dance and movement for your youngsters a less daunting prospect.

First, it's good to remember that you've got an enthusiastic crowd. Children love to move – after all, more often the problem is trying to get them to keep still – and they are completely fascinated with their own bodies. That fascination is a great place to start. It's also interesting to see how aware of their various body parts different children are, and which areas tend to remain a mystery for longer. Why is it that so many children confuse shoulder and elbow? No one knows!

So here's a good warm-up. Get your children down on the floor, on their feet, but scrunched up as small as they can get – yes, you too! Now you must imagine that you are puppets with strings going from the tops of your ears to the ceiling. As the strings start to tighten, you are pulled up to standing. Now imagine that there are strings from your fingertips too, so that your hands extend high above your head. All the strings pull as tight as they can, so that you are on tiptoe and reaching up to the sky. Then suddenly someone comes and cuts the strings and you collapse back down to the floor. Repeat this version several times so the children get used to the process. You can vary with slow motion stretching up and super-fast collapse, or vice versa.

Then start to introduce different body parts. Can they do it with a string attached to their knee? Nose? Elbow? Shoulder? Toe? Bottom?

An aside here…you don't need me to tell you how hilarious bottoms are – across the board! So I always try to include them, but more often than not at the end, as it's sometimes a bit tricky to get the concentration back after all that giggling.

~~~~~~

Talking of bottoms: I invented a potential television show once that was provisionally called 'Where's My Bottom?' (I was later made to change the title – spoilsports.) It was born out of an afternoon looking after a friend's four-year-old. We'd got big sheets of paper on the floor, and having drawn round each other (see last chapter) I followed her lead when she started pointing out body parts, first on her avatar, and then on her own body. Having copied her for a while, I then couldn't resist posing the challenge, 'But where's my bottom?' which led to the two of us running round and round ourselves, like dogs chasing our own tails, trying to see our own behinds, and then falling about laughing on the floor.

It eventually became a song, incorporating many body parts, and if you'd like to use it, here it is:

I know where my hands are.
I can touch my toes.
Look here are my elbows.
But where's my bottom?

Up here are my shoulders.
Round here is my waist.

Down there are my two legs.
But where's my bottom?

I know where my ears are.
Watch me blink my eyes.
See me show my teeth off.
But where's my bottom?

I can flick my fingers.
I can twitch my nose.
Look here is my tummy.
But where's my bottom?

I can put my arms up.
See me stomp my feet.
I can make my knees knock.
But where's my bottom?

See my mouth is massive.
This bit is my tongue.
Look here are my eyebrows.
But where's my bottom?

~~~~~~~~~~

Because we adults have had our bodies for quite a long time now, and have grown rather used to them and where everything is, it's easy to forget that for the children it's all new, and it's changing all the time. There are a couple of little games that, whilst actually just demonstrating some of the ways the body works, come across like magic tricks.

Try this – put one hand in the air (like you just don't care) high above your head, and hang the other as low as it will go. Count to 20 or 30, now look at the backs of your hands together. They may be contrasting colours, and the veins should definitely look different on each hand.

And this – stand in a doorway, arms straight by your sides with palms facing inwards. Keep the arms straight, open them so that the backs of your hands are in touch with the door frame and then press outwardly against the frame. Or if the arm span is too wee for that, then get someone to press inwardly against your wrists as you press outwardly against that pressure, again arms straight and palms facing one another. Hold for around 30 seconds then step away and relax, letting your arms fall to their natural position. You should feel your arms floating up to the sides, unbidden.

Another framework for exploring body parts can lead into an opportunity for broader movement creation.

Start by simply asking them to draw in the air with their fingers. Older children might be able to write their names, but with younger ones you can simplify as necessary, perhaps just drawing their initial(s), or even simple shapes – square, circle, wavy line, and they could try a star for fun. Ask them to draw really big, and then super small. Then ask them to draw with their elbow, nose, toe, knee and bottom last, of course.

You can then turn this into a 'Story of Me' dance by asking the children to add on movements for their favourite animal, pastime, story, TV character and so on. This can also be a fun development of the activity with the paper puppet of themselves described in the last chapter.

Some children will struggle with physical recall, finding it difficult to replicate movements they have previously created and executed. Like most things, this is a skill that gets better with practice, and you can help with an easy memory game. A simple somatic version of 'I went to the market and I bought a...' will do perfectly. Stand in a circle, so everyone can see one another nice and clearly. I would recommend a verbal repetitive hook to hang the activity on, so everyone knows whose turn it is, and to set up a nice rhythm; you may even want to clap out a tempo. Something like, 'Nikky's move is this...1–2–3,' then the next player will copy and add their own move to the previous child's, 'Nikky's move is this...1–2–3. Joe's move is this...1–2–3.' You may need a few attempts before it runs smoothly, but the children should pick up the process in time. Stress (and model) that the moves must be super simple and short, jumps, stamps, nods, a spin, etc., to fit with the 1–2–3 timing.

It takes time for small children to learn how to work collaboratively, and trying to get them to co-operate in a co-ordinated whole group activity can be a big ask. However, movement games are a fabulous way to encourage them to work together. One of my favourites involves nothing more complex than a couple of straws. The children work in pairs and stand facing each other balancing the straws between the palms of their hands. For the very little ones, this can be enough of a challenge in itself. The next stage is to see if they can move their hands up and down, as one. Then they can try out to the sides and back in, push and pull, and for the very ambitious, drawing circles or lowering all the way to the floor and back up to standing. If they master that easily, try it with the straw balanced only between fingertips.

Most nurseries will have a selection of beanie babies, or even just plain bean bags. These can be used for individuals to try and balance on different bits of their bodies – whilst standing still, or moving around – or indeed for pairs of children to pass to one another, knee to knee, foot to foot, or back of hand to back of hand, for example.

If your children are reasonably physically capable, you can get them sitting back to back on the floor, practising leaning onto one another to gently take each other's weight. The ultimate goal is for them to be able to stand up and sit down again remaining in contact.

It's true that chaos can ensue when you have a hall full of small children, overexcited with the prospect of being allowed to dance about in a big space. To help with this, I designate areas of the room into a Thinking Place and a Doing Space. Sometimes this description alone is enough, at other times I might name them Backstage and Performance Area, Recharge and Energise, or Secret Planning and Shared Action or similar – you get the idea.

The premise behind the practice is that you use the geography of the area in which you are working to order the behaviour of the children. When calling them back to the (let's settle on this one example for now) Thinking Place, you can give your instructions for what you want them to do next in the voluminous expanse of the rest of the room – but not quite yet. I like to huddle them around me as closely as possible and give my directions as if it were a confidential meeting amongst spies. Exciting and conspiratorial. In that way, you build anticipation for the moment when they will be allowed to invade the open space with their movement invention, but there is also an attraction to coming back to 'base' for the next secret disclosure.

It's up to you what themes you deal with in these sessions, but here are some of my favourite suggestions to prompt their movement.

- Weather:

  ◦ Rain – tippy-tappy fingers, rain falling, puddle splashing, sheltering.

  ◦ Wind – breeze, leaf blowing, stronger, blowing away, tree in gale.

  ◦ Sun – ball of fire, radiating out, feeling heat, mirage.

  ◦ Snow – snowflakes landing on different parts, shivering, footprints, snow angels.

- Animals small to big:

  ◦ Flies, spiders, worms, birds, cats, dogs, horses, elephants – do these one at a time, then have a grand finale where they work their way down from elephant to fly, all in one go.

- Household machines:
  - Washing machine, kettle, microwave, iron, toaster, lawnmower, clock.

- Superpowers:
  - Flying, being able to grow extra big/extra small, moving things with psychic force, being invisible.

These are only a few examples and you can build on these ideas as you see fit. I choose to call the children back between each suggestion and then have a final session where they can really let rip, incorporating all their ideas up to that point. You may or may not want to use music to accompany your class movement sessions, but may I just give a hint that if you do, it may be helpful to hold your children in the Thinking Place to listen a little, and maybe discuss, before they are set free to dance to it in the Doing Space. Of course, slow and minimal music can be your friend when you want to calm down your class at the end of any movement session. For myself, I like to finish by having the children lie on the floor for a short period of relaxation and visualisation, concentrating on breathing slowly and deeply, to help them calm down at the end.

You may well have children in your class who are quite restrained or shy, or who may be, for whatever reason, lacking in physical confidence. I've always found the best way to deal with this is not to apply any pressure, to be patient and to wait until the child feels ready to join in. If they never do, this may be an issue to address with parents or professionals, but don't rush the issue; some of us just take longer to feel comfortable with bodily expression.

~~~~~~~~~~

Whilst working in children's television, I was tasked with creating a movement segment to fit into an already existing show, which was to be sold into the American market. The brief was essentially to encourage children to perform short moves demonstrating their physical prowess, and that these demonstrations should be so irresistible as to entice the viewer off the couch to join in with the child on the television.

In order to achieve this, I felt I needed to find children with physical skills across the board. So I not only visited regular schools, but also dance schools, martial arts centres, gymnastic clubs, and sports halls as well as including children with SEN.

Patience was everything, and having gone along to observe and introduce myself, I then invited everyone along to what was billed as a movement workshop. (I'm not a fan of holding 'auditions' for young children, it doesn't seem fair – much better to just hold a fun and play-filled session that everyone involved might enjoy.)

Building on the practice in my school work of designating specific areas, I travelled with a large, bright red vinyl spot approximately five feet in diameter. After a brief warm-up we would settle down to the task in hand. All participating children would sit on the floor around the big red circle and I would explain that the game was called 'Look What I Can Do!' Unless a particularly brave child would step forward as first candidate (and that was unusual) I would model the procedure by stepping onto the red circle and repeatedly demonstrating a simple movement. Everyone else was then invited to get up and join in with that movement, until it felt that it had run its course, when we would all retake our seats around the circle until the next player felt courageous enough to get up and take the stage.

The groups of around 8–12 children would variously take to the game, some wanting to have repeated turns – so that you'd have to hold them back somewhat in order to let another person have a go – and others who would refuse repeated invitations to participate. The latter kind of child was always interesting. I never pressurised them, just checked if they'd like a turn yet, and when they declined, just moved on without fuss. In every group I worked with, that reluctant child would, when you least expected it (and generally some way towards the end of the session), suddenly leap up and take the stage, performing something truly intriguing. Once the seal was broken, there'd be no stopping them, and it was always that child who would be protesting that they wanted to play more as we were trying to pack up and leave.

I'd also like to state that in some schools it was the so-called 'naughty boys' who really excelled themselves in this activity. Sometimes a child just needs the opportunity to shine in a field that suits them, and that field may not be the traditionally academic.

~~~~~~~~~~~~~~

There's a proviso to the activities above that make use of a specifically denoted space. I've occasionally been asked to hold movement workshops where the children have been pre-prepared for me by being neatly arranged in a hall space, each one standing on a small coloured disc, having been instructed not to move off this disc during the whole PE class. I don't like this. In my own use of designating space, there is always an option open to the child, and the rigidity of 'Stay on the spot!' doesn't give that option. For a bunch of people who are almost always desperate to be free to express themselves physically, it seems terribly unfair to say to them, 'Here's the time we've given you for that free physical expression, but only in that tiny area…that tiny area there…don't go beyond that tiny area with your free movement…' That just seems wrong to me.

After all, for such body-centric little beings, physicality should be a way for them to develop increased confidence rather than to realise the potential for untold neuroses in the future.

You may have come across Amy Cuddy's TED Talk (if not then do google and have a look – it's worth a watch) where she explains the positive mental impact of spending two minutes adopting a powerful physical position, such as the arms aloft in a 'V' shape stance that we all recognise, and indeed instinctively adopt ourselves, as a sign of victory when breaking the tape at the end of a race. For young children who are mostly lacking in physical inhibition, it's a relatively easy step to encourage them to feel positive about themselves, to express that positive feeling with their bodies and, therefore in turn, according to Professor Cuddy, increase their chances of success in whatever task then lies ahead.

I am a great believer in the link between body and mind. I don't think that our bodies are merely vessels for transporting our brains from place to place – au contraire, I think that our brains developed in order to effectively control and work with the complexity of our physiology. We are still a long way from completely understanding how our minds and bodies work. Until recently, when scientists cut open human beings in order to examine them, they merely tossed the fascia aside, as something in the way of the important stuff, but now we are starting to discover what a vital role this under-the-skin wetsuit of tissue plays in our muscular and skeletal well-being. My point is that our knowledge of our own biology is changing and growing all the time, so I feel we are duty bound to help our future generations develop as close and as mutually respectful a relationship between brain and body as is possible.

As for us in our roles as teachers, we also need to be mindful of our own health – physically and mentally – but that's the next chapter.

THE KERNELS

- Children are almost always endlessly fascinated by their own bodies. It's never too early to build on that to increase their knowledge of and respect for their own physicality.

- Be a good audience – praise and applaud every effort they make.

- Brain and body are not separate, they work in conjunction, so create challenges for the whole being.

Chapter 11

TAKING CARE

Your well-being really matters too, so here are some suggestions for looking after yourself, so that you can look after the children even better.

It should be acknowledged that not just taking care of, but also purposefully stimulating and educating young children, can be jolly hard work. We are trying to keep up with little bundles of energy who are hard-wired to be investigating as much as possible, as often as possible. Plenty of attention is given to trying to keep our children healthy – making sure they eat properly, trying to ensure they get enough rest, as well as plenty of exercise and fresh air – but sometimes the well-being of those adults doing the tough job of dealing with children's needs all day can be overlooked.

Earlier, I suggested some exercises you can do to help you protect your voice, but equally you will benefit from looking after your body too. From a performer's point of view, when you're given any new role, part and parcel of the preparation is examining the physical demands that may be made of you, and making sure you are all trained up in order to pull them off. Not only because that's your job, but also so that you are minimising risk of injuring, damaging or just plain exhausting yourself.

So for one week at work, take a notebook, put it in your mind to pay attention to the physical exertions of your job, observe your colleagues too, and take a few notes. What are the movements that you are repeating most often? What less frequent but more extreme demands are put on your body? Do you notice any occasions where you're unable to rely on your body to do want you want? Are there restrictions in your range of motion (when looking behind you, for example) or in your stamina? What makes you tired?

Have conversations with your colleagues and swap notes; you may be able to support each other in your bid to be as fit for your job as possible. There are personal trainers and body workers such as yoga and Pilates teachers who are often happy to come to a place of work to hold one-off or regular sessions, specifically designed to meet your needs. Yes, I know time is always tight, but there really isn't anything more crucial than looking after yourself. The received wisdom is that you should chose some form of exercise that you enjoy doing, so that it doesn't become a hideous chore, and find a form that suits you. Take into account whether you like being with other people or would value some time alone, whether you like silence, musical accompaniment or would prefer the chance for a chat.

The good news is that once you start, the tendency is that the more you do, the more you are motivated to do, and that will only benefit you and your children.

So, once you have your notes, you should be able to pick out patterns, which will indicate where you need to build strength or increase flexibility. You can use this information to help decide which kind of exercise will be most advantageous to you, and also pass it on to any professional you may invite in. If there are enough of you who are interested, you could approach your leadership team and ask for some CPD (Continuing Professional Development) to enhance the physical fitness of the staff.

In short – examine what you do, and train for that.

The really wonderful thing about keeping yourself fit is that it opens up options to you. I have worked with some excellent EYFS practitioners who were sedentary most of the time. They were very good teachers, but I know they would have been even better had they been able to get up and move about with the children a bit more. Some of the advantages for the children are incredibly basic.

I was working with a reception class and during one break time when all the other children were outside playing, one little boy came up to me whilst I was tidying up, and started talking about how apprehensive he was about his imminent move to year one. We sat on the carpet together for the whole of break and I'm glad to say that by the end, he was feeling a lot more secure and most of his fears had been allayed. The first child back into the classroom was a lovely bouncy little girl who rocked right up to me and declared accusingly, 'What are YOU doing on the floor, Miss, you're a grown-up!'

So struck was I by this, that I'm not even sure I offered a response. I was just overwhelmed by the thought that no adult in this little girl's life ever got down and spoke to her eye to eye. No one got down on the floor, to her level, ever. Not her teacher, not her parents, not any other adult she ever came into contact with at all. As far as she was concerned the floor was purely a kids zone and grown-ups just didn't make the effort to visit. Apart from the psychological impact of having to look upwards all the time to anyone already raised in a position of authority, the physiological damage to her skeleton, and the cervical spine in particular, will keep a fair few therapists in gainful employ in the future. Try it yourself; it doesn't take long to feel how uncomfortable that is. I know it's bound to happen some of the time, it's part of the package of being a small person, but we can stop it being the norm by just bending down or squatting a bit more often.

There may also be an opportunity to make life easier for yourself by adjusting your environment. Naturally, the layout of most classrooms will prioritise the movement patterns of largish groups of children, and will be, quite sensibly, zoned off into different areas catering for different activities. But there may be slight alterations you can make that could result in bigger changes. What about the height of your main chair? Where does the light fall? If you have a board to refer to, is it easy to turn between it and the children? Where do you keep your things? Are you able to reach everything easily? The questions will vary depending on your situation, but just taking a little time to make sure that the environment suits you as best as possible, as well as the children, could prevent aches, pains and fatigue in the future.

You don't really need me to tell you how to take care of yourself from day to day, and I do understand how difficult and how jam-packed with events, both planned and unpredicted, a day can be. But I've known so many school workers who don't have lunch, or who just manage to snack on half a slice of toast at some point – I've done it myself many times, and it's just not good. So all I'm saying is TRY to take some time for you. Eat. Sleep. Get Fresh Air. Look After Yourself. Well – you know the drill. It just takes a bit of extra effort to get into a healthier routine. Once you're there, it's much easier, and if you're already there, you have my undying admiration!

In addition to the outside demands that everyone working in education is familiar with, I think we can tend to put an undue amount of pressure on ourselves. What I have seen over and over again, in decades of promoting creative teaching and learning practice, is a tendency for teachers to take it all on themselves. A phrase I often find myself using is 'Where is the creativity?' and often there is a member of staff working themselves into the ground, pulling out the stops, all the bells and whistles, but *they* are where the creativity is sitting – it's not necessarily with the children.

Life is not a cabaret, and your lessons certainly shouldn't be. Make sure that the creativity is not all on your side, and that the majority of the effort is being made by the children, not you.

In my own practice I err on the side of expecting a lot of my children. Having high expectations of your children is a strong motivator for them to strive to achieve and is, after all, evidence to them that you believe that they are capable of great things. Often, you have more belief in them than they have in themselves, and they *will* want to live up to that expectation rather than let you down.

Obviously this is a bit of a generalisation. It will not be true, in the same way, for every single child, so it will be up to you to know your children well enough to temper your communications sensitively.

Your two greatest allies in this balancing act are observation and reflection. When you are looking at your children, don't just focus on *what* they are doing, take in *how* they are doing it too. Check out their body language to see how they really feel about what they are doing and who they are doing it with. If you notice that a certain child has a very particular way of holding themselves, a definite repertoire of moves that they regularly repeat, or a specific way of moving about – try copying it. Not right in front of them of course! But subtly find a place where you can try to mimic as closely as possible what they are doing with their bodies. It can really tell you a lot about what's going on in their minds.

Even if you don't take it this far (but you should), do employ that Full Body Listening, especially if you're only dealing with one or two children. Get as close to eye level as you can and take in as much information as you are able, not just what they are saying but also how they are saying it, timbre, pitch, volume, choice of language; the intricacies of their facial expressions and how they are using their bodies, their heads, their gaze and focus; how they are moving their eyes and the overall picture – if you soften your own visual focus what is the picture you see?

As an actress and puppeteer, I have had to really hone my observation skills, in order to believably replicate various human behaviours and traits, either with my own person or with a puppet. Little did I know at the time how incredibly useful those skills would be when my workplace shifted to a classroom.

There are plenty of books written on the subject of observation, so I'm not going to go into more detail here, but what I would like to say – keeping with the theme of the chapter – is that it doesn't have to be just you doing the observing.

Schools will often want to promote a certain set of values or behaviours, and I have often used this as a way-in to train my own little army of spies! For example, if the focus for that week, month, term, or whatever is 'Working Collaboratively', then once the majority of the children have a handle on what that means, you can set up a game I like to call 'Learning Detectives'. All that needs to happen is that you encourage the children to keep an eye out, all the time, for when they see one another Working Collaboratively – or whatever the focus happens to be. Once the desired behaviour is spotted, then both the child or children exhibiting the behaviour *and* the Learning Detectives who spotted it are praised to the heavens. If you like, you can appoint specific Learning Detectives for limited amounts of time and then let them take turns. I've always found this framework really successful and helpful – it gets the children used to paying attention to how each other are acting in the classroom, and what they are learning.

This feeds into your other ally: reflection.

It can be hugely beneficial for children to know what they have been learning and why it might be important. Depending on the context, it may be valuable to let them know the what and the why before the activity takes place. This is especially true of the more academic end of the EYFS requirements. However, it is pretty much always of value to put aside some time after an activity, or at the end of the morning, the afternoon, or the day, in order to discuss what's gone on whilst the children have been with you.

There are many ways of doing this. There are plenty of suggestions and reflection tools and resources available online and elsewhere. Photography and learning journals can be useful, as can getting the children to actually physicalise whether or not they enjoyed an activity – this side of the room for yes, the other side for no, and then all points in between for the various levels of maybe. However, I think it's most informative if you just have a little chat. There may have been things you've observed that you'd like to ask the children about. Do they have anything they want to discuss?

The important thing is that you are trying to draw out of them their own analysis of what has occurred.

Why did they do such and such a thing? What can they remember from their time with you? Can they identify any specific achievements? What are they proud of? What was disappointing? … And so on.

Once again, if I draw an analogue with the life of a performer, I know that there is an awful lot gained from the support you get from working as part of a company, part of a team. I spoke at the beginning about the benefits of creating that sense of togetherness in the classroom, and here's a story of when it really paid dividends.

~~~~~~~~~~~

The room was large and open plan, housing two reception classes of around 30 children each. The two classes had their own base at either end of the space, but the children were often able to mingle and cross-fertilise, especially during free play sessions. There was also a small room attached for when some privacy or special focus was needed for a particular child or group of children. They were also lucky enough to have an outside space, with the tarmac area under cover and grass beyond.

The school wanted to implement a new and freer planning regime so that future teaching could be directly built on what had recently happened in the classroom, to try and give the children some continuity. This was also an attempt to consolidate the staff. The two teachers and four job-sharing TAs (Teaching Assistants) were not happy as a team. The TAs felt that they were under-used and spent too much time 'glue-pot washing' rather than being asked to draw on the wealth of knowledge they had accumulated over many years' experience in education. The teachers felt that the amount of paperwork, evidence and assessment they were expected to produce was overwhelming and that they didn't have enough time in the day to really organise and work with their team.

During a staff training day, the whole reception staff were given time to get together and come up with a plan. They decided that the TAs would take responsibility for pupil observation and evidence gathering. It didn't need to be ornate or burdensome; in fact, they were encouraged to take photographs and make a brief record on a post-it note whenever they were struck by a child's particular behaviour or achievement. They then put the notes in a designated box on the class teacher's desk.

At the end of the day, the whole class team would get together to review the photos and notes, and from that information, an outline plan would be agreed for the next day. It took a little time for them to really get into the groove, but before long their after-school planning talks got down to around 15–20 minutes, including processing the photographs. Despite the TAs only being paid up until the end of the children's school day, the increase in their level of responsibility was sufficient reward for them to put in that little bit of extra time.

They produced individual books for each child into which they could transfer the photographs and observation notes. All the staff felt, and worked as, part of a fully functioning team, and the glue pots still got washed – by the children!

It only took some acknowledgement of their ability, and a resulting shift in their role, for those TAs to step up to the plate and give a little more to get a lot more job satisfaction. The whole staff felt they had a team where everyone contributed to the combined effort of giving the children the best possible education for their stage in life. Everyone was much happier.

When things start to get on top of you, it can be harder than ever to see your way clear to delegating effectively – just when you most need it. It's essential to make the most of your team, and to remember that the children are a crucial part of that team. You don't have to do it all yourself. Remember that the children are there to learn, they are *supposed* to be doing the work – hand it over to them whenever you possibly can.

I do believe that it's a real privilege to be able to work with young children. They are incredibly important, and that's why you are incredibly important. You are doing a great thing in shaping future generations, and you clearly want to be the best you can be at it, or you wouldn't have bothered to read this book – and now you're nearly at the end.

What you do in the theatre of your classroom is much more critical than just trying to please an audience. You work on the most important stage there is, so go and nail that performance.

Break a leg!

THE KERNELS

- Look after yourself – you need to be fit in order to best serve your children.

- Who's doing the work? Make sure the creativity is with them and not just with you.

- Have Great Expectations.

Chapter 12

THE GOLDEN RULES

A summary of top tips and reminders from the checklists at the end of each chapter.

It's not that easy to summarise everything I've covered in ten handy home hints, but I've done my best here to get to the heart of the matter and deal with core values rather than specifics – as there are plenty of those in the preceding chapters. I hope you've found this book helpful to your continuing career in EYFS. It's been a pleasure to write, and I hope also to read. Happy teaching!

- **Be True to Yourself** – We all have different styles in the classroom. All you can do is to be honest; it really is the best policy.

- **Put Yourself in Their Position** – Literally and metaphorically, in any situation, have a good think about how things look from their perspective.

- **Free Your Mind** – You are in the delightful position of being able to be playful in your job. Yes, there's the EYFS framework to adhere to, but within that, there's plenty of opportunity to let your imagination run wild.

- **Get Them Involved** – Wherever you can, let your children be part of the decision making, so they can own the whole process.

- **Listen to Them** – The biggest gripe I hear from children is that they are not listened to properly, so do it with your whole self and really pay attention; they will tell you everything you need to know.

- **Follow Their Lead** – Go to each individual as you find them, not to what you've been told about them, and let their conduct dictate your behaviour.

- **Commit** – Mean everything 100 per cent.

- **Look After Yourself** – The fuller the life you lead outside the classroom, the more resources you have to draw upon when you're in it.

- **Praise Them** – Often and sincerely.

- **Have Fun!** – If you enjoy yourself, then your children will enjoy themselves, and a happy child is a learning child.

Index

desire lines 30–1
from children's perspective 31
and self-care 136–7
study/analyse 30–1
physical interruptions,
  embedding 36
physicality of young children 29,
  33–4, 36, 119–20
praise 23
prediction, repetition and 88–9
puppets
  'dolly waggling' 110
  masks 116
  observation and 111
  power of 109–10
  and PSE 115
  as representational selves 115
  space traveller story 112
  to enhance storytelling 111–2
  used by the children 116

reflection (children's) 140–1
rehearsals 22
repetition, prediction and 88–9
rituals 21, 78
role models 17
role play
  aims of 56
  deciding the theme 57, 60
  duration of 59–60
  involving children in decisions
    about 57–8
  staff participation 60–1
  structure of 56
  tick-box approach to 55
  train theme (example) 58–9
roles, giving to children 22
routine
  importance of 21–2

including ritual in 78
  procedures 38–9

seaside sensory journey 51–4
'Secret Life of Objects' stories
  102
self-belief 16
self-care
  adjustments to physical
    environment 136–7
  attending to physical exertions
    134–5
  ensuring majority of effort
    from children 137–8, 143
  finding own strategies for
    25–6
senses
  hearing 44–5
  'sensory journey' 50–4
  smell 47–8
  taste 49–50
  touch 46–7
  vision 42–4
shyness 127–8
signs, inventing 90–1
silent time 37
singing 78
special needs children 31
spot, staying on the 33–4, 130
stop signal, conductor's 80
'Story of Me' dance 123–4
storytelling
  adding extra expression to 99
  committing to the story 96
  creating your own story 100–1
  enhanced by puppets 111–2
  fairytales 102–4
  importance of 108
  leaving gaps 98, 101